STRATEGIC LEADERSHIP: REALIZING STUDENT ASPIRATION OUTCOMES

STRATEGIC LEADERSHIP: REALIZING STUDENT ASPIRATION OUTCOMES

INAS ZULKIPLI PH.D.
HAIRUDDIN MOHD ALI PH.D.

PARTRIDGE

Library of Congress Control Number: 2018957264
ISBN: Softcover   978-1-5437-4780-5
                eBook   978-1-5437-4779-9

To order additional copies of this book, contact
Toll Free 800 101 2657 (Singapore)
Toll Free 1 800 81 7340 (Malaysia)
orders.singapore@partridgepublishing.com

www.partridgepublishing.com/singapore

TABLE OF CONTENTS

LIST OF TABLES

PREFACE

Salam and cheerful greetings to everybody, the readers, postgraduate students, researchers, educators, educational managers and leaders, and scholars.

This book titled "Strategic Leadership: Realizing Student Aspiration Outcomes" is solidly a research based book originated from a PhD thesis, a comprehensive study by the first author and supervised by the second author. Due to lacking of contemporary knowledge in educational strategic leadership and management, this book is definitely able to contribute considerably to the present literature.

Altogether, there are eight separate chapters comprising: Chapter One (Background of Malaysian Education System), Chapter Two (The Upper Echelons Theory and Strategic Leadership Practices), Chapter 3 (Organizational Bureaucracy), Chapter Four (In-service Training Effectiveness), Chapter 5 (Students' Aspiration Outcomes), Chapter Six (How the Research was Conducted), Chapter 7 (Descriptive Analysis of the Sample Data), and Chapter 8 (The Strategic Leadership Practices of Vocational College Leaders: The Way Forward). The readers, scholars and educational fraternity will find that the chapters are arranged in a manner how a comprehensive study was conducted scientifically.

Chapter One (Background of the Malaysian Education System). This chapter describes the background of Malaysian Education System in general and how it develops since the nation gains her independence in 1957. The aim, objectives and the research framework of the study are also outlined in this chapter in such away as a clear road-map in conducting a comprehensive study. **Chapter Two (The Upper Echelons Theory and Strategic Leadership Practices).** This chapter accommodate the main theory uses by the study i.e. The Upper Echelons Theory. The concepts of leadership particularly its applicability in education are also described. The latest literatures are also part of this chapter. **Chapter 3 (Organizational Bureaucracy).** This chapter in particular is about 'Organizational Bureaucracy' which this particular study hypothesized it as a mediator. Organizational bureaucracy is considered pertinent to the administrators in controlling and organizing processes in their management endeavors. But organizational bureaucracy is sometime considered as hindrance to the smoothness of the management processes. Thus this book is trying to highlight how effective this variable acts as a mediator in Malaysian context. The result could be a blow to Malaysian system of administration. **Chapter Four (In-service Training Effectiveness).** This chapter comprises a description of in-service training conducted in Malaysian vocational education system. As one of the staff development endeavors implement by the education system, this book is highlighting it as one of the mediating factors similar to organizational bureaucracy. Thus, this book is trying to justify if in-service training plays as an effective mediator or vice-versa.

Chapter five (Students' Aspiration Outcomes). This chapter tries to highlight what are the students' outcomes as the main condition for Malaysian system of education to become world class education provider. The success and achievements of students' aspirations are the goals of Malaysian Education Blueprint 2013-2025. This book highlights and explains the students' outcomes factors and applies in Malaysian context. **Chapter Six (The Research Methods).** This part highlights how the research study is carried out. Thus aspects such as population, sampling, instrumentation, data analysis and statistical techniques used are clearly explained. **Chapter 7 (Analysis of the Sampled Data and Results).** This chapter is merely discussing how the data collected is analyzed based on the suggestions by the authors. Demographic profiles of the respondents is discussed followed by the analyses and results of various statistical techniques employed. **Chapter 8 (The Strategic Leadership Practices of Vocational College Leaders: The Way Forward).** This is the final chapter of the book which discusses the results of the research, how the results implicate the Malaysian Vocational education sector and last but not least is the recommendations for the concerned education sector for future improvements and sustainability.

With the successful publication of this book, the authors are looking at as many as possible the readers, educational managers and leaders as well as scholars out there are taking the opportunity to enrich their contemporary strategic leadership knowledge transpired from this book and successfully apply them in their future endeavors.

INAS ZULKIPLI & HAIRUDDIN MOHD ALI
AUGUST, 9th. 2018.

CHAPTER ONE

BACKGROUND OF THE MALAYSIAN EDUCATION SYSTEM

The Malaysian education system underwent a few stages of changes since the British occupation. In general, the stages can be divided into five periods: the pre-independence period (before 1957), post-independence period (1957–1970), the New Economic Policy period (1971–1990), the National Development Policy period (1991–2000), and the National Vision Policy period (2001–2010). In each phase, there were significant reformations carried out on the education system.

The Malaysian education system subsisted since before the Independence of Malaya (before 1957). During the British colonization, the education system practices were in-line with the "divide-and-rule" concept imposed by the British. Each race (i.e. the Malays, the Chinese and the Indians) had their schools established using their mother tongues. The curriculum, books and teachers were from the respective races too. The British also established the English schools for all races, but the majority of the people opposed this.

When the British agreed to give independence to Malaya, one of the concerns was to create an integrated education system for all races. Several committees had been established to study the existing education system and produce some relevant reports such as Barnes Report (1951), Fenn-Wu (1951), Education Ordinance (1952) and Razak Report (1956).

The Barnes Report (1951) aimed to review and improve the Malays' education. The Fenn-Wu Report (1951) sought to review the Chinese education system. The Education Ordinance (1952) was produced to recommend the National School concept as the national education system, whereas the Razak Report (1956) aimed to lay a platform for the development of a one-nation education system with the aim of fostering unity. The development included the usage of the Malay language as the medium of instruction, a standardized curriculum and syllabus for all schools.

The second stage of the Malaysian education system was after independence (the period of 1957–1970). During this stage, the government's focus was on the establishment of a national education system. The Education Ordinance 1957 was enacted based on the Razak Report. In 1960, the Rahman Talib Committee reviewed the Razak Report, which led to the enactment of the Education Act 1961. The Education Act outlined the Malay language as the primary medium of instruction at all levels of education and enacted a standardized curriculum and examinations for all students.

During the third stage, from 1971 to 1990, the focus of education was to reduce the imbalance in the society by promoting equal education access for all races. Significant changes in the education system were introduced. These included:

1. Making the Malay language a compulsory medium of instruction in all secondary schools.
2. Maintaining the Chinese and Tamil languagesas the mediums of instruction in the national-type schools.
3. Introducing Civics education as a subject to enhance the national identity.
4. Emphasizing science and technical education to fulfil the labour market needs.

The most significant reform during this period was the establishment of the National Education Philosophy in 1988. The composition was meant to strengthen the aims of the national education system with an emphasis on producing holistic and integrated students.

The fourth stage witnessed rapid changes in the education system starting from 1990. Most of the legal basis for the implementation of the educational policies was enacted during this period, which involved primary, secondary and mostly the tertiary levels of education. The National Education Policy was launched in 1999 and was revised in 2004 and 2012.

The fifth stage, mainly starting from the year 2000, saw the impact of globalization on the Malaysian education system and the rapid demands of the information communication technology (ICT). Thus, while maintaining the holistic and integrated aims of the education system, a new emphasis was added in response to the 21st century's need which was students must be ICT-capable. In line with the objectives of Vision 2020, the Ministry of Education Malaysia (MOEM) had launched a number of education master plans to upgrade the standards of the Malaysian education system. These included:

1. the Education Development Master Plan (PIPP 2006-2010),
2. the Ministry of Education Strategic Interim Plan (2011–2020),
3. the Malaysian Education Development Plan (2013-2025)

THE MALAYSIAN GOVERNMENT'S OFFICIAL EDUCATIONAL DOCUMENTS ON EDUCATION

This section presents four authoritative documents related to the Malaysian education system, i.e. the National Education Philosophy, the National Education Policy, the Education Development Master Plan (PIPP 2006-2010), and the Malaysian Education Development Plan (2013-2025).

The National Education Philosophy

The National Education Philosophy was formulated in 1988 and was revised and stated in the Education Act 1996 (Act 540) as the government's vision ofeducation. The National Education Philosophy states;

> *Education in Malaysia is an on-going effort towards further developing the potential of individuals in a holistic and integrated manner, so as to produce individuals who are intellectual, spiritually, emotionally, and physically balanced and harmonious, based on a firm belief in and devotion to God. Such an effort is designed to produce Malaysian citizens who are knowledgeable and competent, who possess high moral standards, and who are responsible and capable of achieving high levels of personal well-being as well as being able to contribute to the harmony and betterment of the family, the society, and the nation at large.*

The formulation of the National Education Philosophy went through a fairly lengthy process of nation building since independence. Prompted by the Cabinet Report in 1979, the policy was formulated based on three main references, i.e. the Malaysian Declaration of National Philosophy (*Rukun Negara*), the New Economic Policy (1976-1980) and the National Education Policy (KPM, 2001). The essences of the National Philosophy are as follows:

1. Education is a continuous process of efforts,
2. It has to develop individual potentials,
3. This is done in a holistic and integrated manner,
4. It must produce balanced and harmonious human beings, intellectually, spiritually, emotionally and physically, based on a firm belief and devotion to God,
5. It must produce Malaysian citizens who are knowledgeable, competent, with high moral standards, responsible, capable of achieving high level of personal well-being,
6. Citizens who can contribute towards the betterment of the nation and the society.

The National Education Policy

The National Education Policy was launched in 1999 and was revised in 2004 and 2012. Updates and enhancements that were aligned with the new policy enacted the impact of the National Transformation Plan and the Transformation of Education to cater to Vision 2020's aspirations. The National Education Policy outlines implementation strategies for the Malaysian education system that includes national curriculum, co-curriculum, Islamic Education (*Pendidikan Islam*), 1pupil 1sport (*1Murid 1Sukan*), national unity through education and Upholding Bahasa Melayu, Strengthening English language (MBMMBI) (KPM, 2012).

The Education Development Master Plan (PIPP 2006-2010)

PIPP 2006-2010 was launched in parallel with the national mission and was aimed to increase performance and impact on the nation's development. PIPP was geared to achieve the National Mission under the 9th Malaysia Plan, which was to improve knowledge-building capacity, innovation and nurture a first class mentality. With the aim to produce world-class human capital, the Ministry of Education (MOE), through the PIPP, has outlined agendas in the

Plan through two approaches, namely the equality of educational opportunity and excellence in schools. PIPP was implemented through six strategic pillars:

1. Nation-state building
2. Developing human capital
3. Empowering school
4. Bridging the education gap
5. Elevating the teaching profession
6. Higher education excellence (KPM, 2011)

The Malaysian Education Development Plan (2013-2025)

The Malaysian Education Development Plan (2013-2025) was launched on September 6, 2013. The plan aims to achieve three specific objectives:

I.   Understanding the current performance and challenges of the Malaysian education system, with a focus on improving access to education, raising standards (quality), closing achievement gaps (equity), promoting unity amongst students, and maximizing system efficiency

II. Establishing a clear vision and aspirations of individual students and the education system as a whole over the next 13 years

III. Outlining a comprehensive transformation programme for the system, including key changes to the Ministry, which will allow it to meet new demands, and rising expectations, and to ignite and support overall civil service transformation (pg. E-.

The carefully laid out plan can only be a success if the implementation phases are carried out effectively. In this context, the implementers need to have specific knowledge and skills to ensure the success of the plan. The main implementers are the Ministry, JPNs, PPDs and the schools. The four documents above framed the Malaysian education system to the level where it is now. The implementation covers all schools in Malaysia including the Malaysian Vocational Colleges.

THE MALAYSIAN VOCATIONAL COLLEGES

Vocational Colleges (VC) were formerly known as *Sekolah Menengah Teknik* (SMT) before 2012. Under the Strategic Plan for the Vocational Education

Transformation, students who graduated from VCs will be holding a diploma in vocational education from a particular discipline. The transformation of SMT to VC marked significant changes in vocational education especially from the aspect of managing VCs. Table 1.1 illustrates the distribution of VCs in Malaysia.

To date, there are 10,132 schools in Malaysia. Out of that total, 23.44% (2,375) are secondary schools. There is only a single secondary school system in Malaysia i.e. the National Secondary Schools (*Sekolah Menengah Kebangsaan*). Students from various types of primary schools will enter the national secondary schools. There are also alternative schools such as religious schools (*Sekolah Menengah Kebangsaan Agama/Sekolah Agama Bantuan Kerajaan*) as options, but only a small percentage of students opt for it. Upon the completion of the lower secondary school, students also have the option of going to the Malaysian VCs to pursue their studies in the technical and vocational streams.

Table 1.1 Distribution of the Vocational Colleges throughout Malaysia

States	Vocational Colleges
Perlis	2
Kedah	5
Pulau Pinang	5
Perak	10
Selangor	8
Kuala Lumpur	2
Melaka	3
Negeri Sembilan	6
Johor	9
Pahang	7
Kelantan	5
Terengganu	4
Sabah	7
Sarawak	6
Labuan	1
Total	**80**

Source: Vocational and Technical Division,
Ministry of Education Malaysia (2012)

ISSUES IN THE MALAYSIAN EDUCATION SYSTEM

Through the various educational reformations, numerous influential educational documentations have shaped the educational landscape in terms of the policy, managing the system and students' cognitive performance such as the National Educational Philosophy (1988), the National Educational Policy (1999), the Educational Development Master Plan (2006-2010) and the Ministry of Education Strategic Interim Plan (2011-2020). However, the educational aspirations of the previous educational plans have not been achieved, forcing the government to launch a new educational plan.

The most recent educational plan was the Malaysian Education Development Plan (2013-2025) in 2012. The comprehensive educational plan was seen to be the solution to the Malaysian education dilemmas. Apart from the substantially poor students' cognitive performance internationally, the Malaysian Education Development Plan (2013-2025) addresses several issues that have been highlighted by the *Report on Education Reform and Process of Consultation* (2012), including:

1. Quality of teachers
2. Quality of school administrative staff
3. Quality of school
4. Curriculum improvement
5. Multilingual proficiency
6. Post-school job opportunity
7. Parents', private sector's and the community's involvements
8. Resource management
9. The administrative structure of the Ministry of Education.

To solve the recurring problems, the Malaysian Education Development Plan (2013-2025) highlighted two aspiration outcomes as of utmost importance: system aspirations and students' aspiration. The focus of this research is the students' aspiration outcomes. Students' aspiration is a phrase that is frequently used in most educational documentations though the contextual usage of 'students' aspirations' which varies from one educational document to another. Some regard students' aspirations as values such as ambitious goals set by the students. In the context of the Malaysian Education Development Plan (2013-2025), students' aspirations are the educational goals set by the Plan for students. All Malaysian students who undergo the 11 years of compulsory schooling are expected to possess all of the six students' aspirations highlighted by the plan. The six students' aspirations mentioned in the Malaysian Education Development Plan (2013-2025) are knowledge, thinking skills, leadership skills, bilingual proficiency, ethics and spirituality and national identity.

These aspirations were not formulated out of the blue but were the continuation from past educational documents, mainly the National Education Philosophy (1988), the National Education Policy (1999), the Education Development Master Plan (PIPP 2006-2010), the Malaysian Tenth Plan (2011-2015) and the Ministry of Education Strategic Interim Plan (2011–2020). Table 1.2 maps the students' aspiration outcomes outlined in the aforementioned educational plans with reference to the Malaysian Education Development Plan (2013-2025).

All of the above documents were officially launched at the national level and were the main reference during their time. Nonetheless, after various phases of educational reforms, the students' aspirations outcomes were still being highlighted in all the educational documents. It is, therefore, important to study the determinants influencing the success of the students' aspiration outcomes with reference to the Malaysian Education Development Plan (2013-2025). It is hypothesized that three determinants influence students' aspiration outcomes: strategic leadership practices, organizational bureaucracy, and in-service training effectiveness.

Table 1.2 Mapping Students' Aspiration Outcomes
based on the Malaysian Educational Plans

Students' Aspiration Outcomes	Penyata Razak 1956	National Education Philosophy 1988	Dasar Pendidikan Kebangsaan 1999	Pelan Induk Pembangunan Pendidikan 2006–2010	MOE Strategic Interim Plan 2011-2020	Malaysian Education Development Plan 2013-2025
• Knowledge		✓	✓	✓	✓	✓
• Thinking Skills				✓	✓	✓
• Leadership Skills			✓	✓	✓	✓
• Bilingual Proficiency			✓	✓	✓	✓
• National Identity	✓	✓	✓	✓	✓	✓
• Ethics & Spirituality	✓	✓	✓	✓	✓	✓

Source: Penyata Razak (1956), National Education Philosophy (1988), Dasar Pendidikan Kebangsaan (2012), Pelan Induk Pembangunan Pendidikan 2006-2010 (2006), MOE Strategic Interim Plan 2011-2020 (2011), Malaysian Education Development Plan 2013-2025 (2013)

The first determinant that is hypothesized to influence students' aspiration outcomes and acts as the independent variable in this study is the strategic leadership practices. As widely agreed by educational administrators, strategic leadership practices lead to the success of schools' operation. Research has proven that the development of quality leaders will produce the best possible outcomes of schools' performance. For instance, according to Cuban (1988), "leaders are people who shape the goals, motivations, and actions of others. Frequently they initiate change to reach existing and new goal… Leadership … takes … much ingenuity, energy and skill … (p. 193).

Various educational leadership styles have been proposed. For instance, Bush (2003) identifies several leadership styles as educational leadership styles. These include managerial, transactional, participative/democratic, post-modern, transformational, interpersonal, contingency, instructional, ethical, and strategic leadership. Most of the other leadership styles focus more on the interpersonal characteristics (i.e. what particular characteristics a leader should have), unlike the strategic leadership theories, which consider both the individual traits and the organizational climate as the basis of arguments. Moreover, among all the leadership styles, research on leadership that focuses on top management (i.e. in this context, the school leaders) conventionally embarks on strategic leadership style.

There are several ways to define strategic leadership. Traditionally, strategic leadership refers to the act of determining where an organization was heading and how to get there. More recently, Hughes and Beatty (2005) define strategic leadership as the way of thinking, acting and influencing that promote the competitiveness of an organization. Cheng (2000) stresses the fact that when leaders are involved in the management processes such as analysing, planning, implementing, monitoring and evaluating, they are considered as being strategic. Most strategic leadership definitions incorporate either the characteristics of a strategic leader or the characteristics of a strategic organization. However, Davies and Davies (2004; 2009) combine both characteristics and come up with a strategic leadership model.

According to Davies and Davies (2004; 2009), strategic leadership consists of the characteristics of strategic leaders and their actions (i.e. decision-making) as leaders. Thus, the strategic leadership model proposed by Davies and Davies (2004; 2009) has two constructs: organizational characteristics and individual capabilities. The former includes strategic orientation, strategic translation, strategic alignment, strategic intervention and strategic competencies, whereas the latter consists of restlessness, absorptive capacity, adaptive capacity, and wisdom.

The second determinant that is hypothesized as a mediating variable is organizational bureaucracy. According to the bureaucratic theory of Max Weber, bureaucracy is seen as affecting the office process within an organizations (Hall, 1961). The extent of bureaucracy in an organization reflects human actions and regulates people's freedom (Yucel, 1999).

To measure the extent of organizational bureaucracy on the relationship between strategic leadership and organizational success, Hall (1961) developed an instrument consisting of six variables, i.e. hierarchy of authority, division of labour, rule enforcement, procedural specification, impersonality and technical competence. However, the effect of organizational bureaucracy on students' performance is empirically inconsistent. For example, Meier et al. (2000) found that bureaucracy has little impact on students' performance, while Smith and Lariner (2004) prove that bureaucracy affects school performance. On the other hand, Bohte (2001) reveals that negative relationships exist between bureaucracy and students' performance.

The third hypothesized determinant and the second mediating variable is the in-service training effectiveness. In-service training is a crucial element in an organization. As the nature of an organization is dynamic, its in-service training needs to be continuous. However, research in CPD has discovered an enormous mismatch between training and the actual needs of the recipients (Pedder & Opfer, 2010). The mismatch clearly disturbs the cycle of CPD and most importantly affects the students' performances. According to Harris et al. (2010), the impact of CPD on student learning has received little attention. Figure 1.1 conceptualizes the relationship between the four variables - strategic leadership practices, organizational bureaucracy, in-service training effectiveness and the Malaysian Development Education Plan's students' aspiration outcomes.

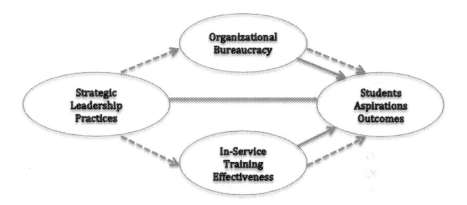

Figure 1.1. The relationship between strategic leadership practices, organizational bureaucracy, in-service training effectiveness and the Malaysian Development Education Plan's students' aspiration outcomes

Based on the above conceptual framework, the main purpose of the study is to examine the relationship between strategic leadership practices in education on students' aspiration outcomes. The specific objectives are to examine:

1. the level of strategic leadership practices, the level of organizational bureaucracy, in-service training's effectiveness and level of students' aspiration outcomes perceived by vocational college leaders.
2. if the measurement model of strategic leadership practices, organizational bureaucracy, in-service training effectiveness and students' aspiration outcomes are valid and reliable.

In other words, the study seeks to determine if:

1. There is a direct and significant relationship between strategic leadership practices and students' aspiration outcomes.
2. There is a direct and significant relationship between organizational bureaucracy and students' aspiration outcomes.
3. There is a direct and significant relationship between in-service training effectiveness and students' aspiration outcomes.

4. Organizational bureaucracy mediates the relationship between strategic leadership practices and students' aspiration outcomes.
5. In-service training effectiveness mediates the relationship between strategic leadership practices and students' aspiration outcomes.
6. The hypothesized model of the study is valid and reliable.

These objectives are translated into the following research questions:

1. What is the level of strategic leadership practices, the level of organizational bureaucracy, in-service training effectiveness and the level of students' aspiration outcomes perceived by vocational college leaders?
2. Is the strategic leadership practices measurement model valid and reliable?
3. Is the level of organizational bureaucracy measurement model valid and reliable?
4. Is the in-service training effectiveness measurement model valid and reliable?
5. Is the students' aspiration outcomes measurement model valid and reliable?
6. Is there a direct and significant relationship between strategic leadership practices and students' aspiration outcomes?
7. Is there a direct and significant relationship between organizational bureaucracy and students' aspiration outcomes?
8. Is there a direct and significant relationship between in-service training effectiveness and students' aspiration outcomes?
9. Does organizational bureaucracy mediate the relationship between strategic leadership practices and students' aspiration outcomes?
10. Does in-service training effectiveness mediate the relationship between strategic leadership practices and students' aspiration outcomes?
11. Is the revised hypothesized structural equation model valid and reliable?

The findings of the study are expected to contribute theoretically and practically to the body of knowledge regarding the Malaysian Vocational Education System. Theoretically, this research is the first study in Malaysia that combines strategic leadership practices, students' aspiration outcomes, organizational bureaucracy and in-service training effectiveness as the variables. Due to the large sample size, the generalizability of the strategic leadership practices among the Malaysian Vocational College leaders can be concluded and has the potential to be developed as the 'strategic leadership practices inventory' for Malaysian school leaders across various school types. In addition, the generalizability of the self-developed students' aspiration outcomes instrument can be claimed to be the current level of students' aspirations with regard to Malaysian Vocational Colleges. The validated instrument can be used to measure the current level of students' aspirations across national-type schools. If the hypothesized mediating variables significantly mediate the relationship between strategic leadership practices and students' aspiration outcomes, we have found statistically significant proof that organizational bureaucracy and in-service training effectiveness influence the success of the Malaysian Education Development Plan (2013-2025).

In terms of practical implications, the above findings will present the exact landscape of the current situation in Malaysian Vocational Colleges in terms of the strategic leadership traits required by the school leaders, the extent of the occurrence of organizational bureaucracy, the perceptions of vocational school leaders towards in-service training and the present level of students' aspiration outcomes with respect to the Malaysian Education Development Plan (2013-2025). Thus, it guides the Technical and Vocational Education Division, Ministry of Education Malaysia to take adequate measures in addressing issues with regard to these research findings.

CHAPTER TWO

THE UPPER ECHELONS THEORY AND STRATEGIC LEADERSHIP PRACTICES

INTRODUCTION

This chapter presents pertinent studies on leadership. It begins with the Upper Echelons Theory which has been widely cited in strategic leadership research. It then delves into the concept of educational leadership, types of leadership related to education, characteristics of strategic leadership and instruments that have been employed to measure leadership. The chapter ends with a discussion of leadership from the Islamic perspective.

THE UPPER ECHELONS THEORY (UET)

The Upper Echelons Theory (UET) was first mentioned in Child's (1972) research. In general, the theory states that the top management actions are based on their personalized interpretations of the situations and the options they have, based on their experiences, personalities, and values that are then translated into their behaviours. Those actions impact the organization's performance. In other words, UET suggests that the knowledge, experiences, and expertise of the individuals occupying managerial roles in the organization directly influence the organizational outcomes (Hambrick & Mason, 1984). UET argues that organizational outcomes, to some degree, can be predicted based on the characteristics of the managers. The theory has been expanded in the work of Hambrick and Mason (1984) and has been widely cited in the strategic leadership research (Canella & Monroe, 1997; Finkelstein & Hambrick, 1996).

Hambrick and Mason (1984) expand the theory by first focusing on the CEOs' background and demographic characteristics. The variables under study include age, career advancement, academic qualification, and socio-economic background. However, limited proof was found in predicting CEOs' strategic decision-making styles and performance using only the demographic variables. Since then, the field of strategic leadership has been concerned only with top-level managers' behaviours, and on strategy formulation and firm performance.

Figure 2.1 shows the UET's perspective on the organization. It describes the elements involved in an organization that starts with the objectives, the characteristics of a leader, strategic choices and elements that directly influence performance. The figure shows that strategic choices made by the leader impact the organization's success.

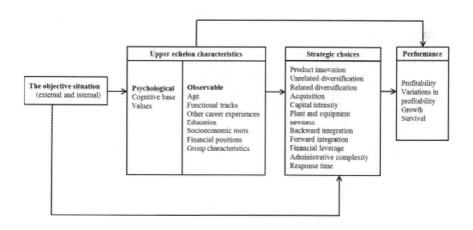

Source: Hambrick & Mason (1984:198)

Figure 2.1 The UET Perspective on Organization

STRATEGIC LEADERSHIP PRACTICES

The Concept of Educational Leadership: Teachers as Leaders

Some scholars believe that research in educational leadership has not been carried out in-depth compared to other educational research. Donmoyer (2011) argues that research in educational leadership field are not equally treated as an academic discipline compared to other subjects like chemistry, or medicine or engineering. Gorard (2005) reveals that most educational leadership research compared to other educational research were done on a smaller scale, resulting in little information provided and some bias. Gorard (2005) further argues that a limited number high-impact journal on educational leadership indicate the non-impact of research in the field. Theoretical development of educational leadership is on-going, but not through empirical-oriented studies (Evers, 2010).

Despite the lack of attention given to educational leadership, research has empirically proven that the role of a school leader influences schools' effectiveness and school leadership and it correlates highly with school performance (Sammons et al., 1997; Levine & Lezotte, 1990; Teddlie & Stringfield, 2003; Scheerens & Bosker, 1997). A famous quote by Huber (1997) states "school leaders matter, they are educationally significant; school leaders do make a difference" (Huber, 1997).

Research also suggests that successful school leaders influence students' achievement through their influence on other people and their impact on school processes. School leaders play multiple roles that make the functions complex and interrelated. Some tasks are related to humans, and some are related to managing resources (Huber, 1997). Rosenbusch (1997) discusses the principles of school leadership as follows:

1. Adjusting school leaders' educational perspective to focus on educational goals over administrative requirements.
2. Dealing with two levels of educational work: school leaders have to deal with children in promoting learning and working with adults and support adult education.
3. Being more resource-oriented to promote strengths instead of counting weaknesses.

4. Following the 'logic of trusting oneself and others': in matters of empowerment, delegation of power, and decision-making. Then, mistakes can be addressed more openly.
5. Respecting and appreciating individuals, and mutual responsibilities with particular emphasis on shared responsibility regarding the common goals.

As most research found the correlation between school leadership and school performance, this research focuses on one specific school leadership style, i.e. strategic leadership of school administrators with the same assumption that it has a direct influence on students' performance. The next subsection briefly discusses the types of educational leadership styles among school leaders.

Types of Leadership Related to Education

Many new leadership models and leadership paradigms have emerged from influential scholars. These include situational leadership, instructional leadership, transformational leadership, servant leadership and strategic leadership. Each of these leadership styles is discussed below.

Situational Leadership

Paul Hersey and Kenneth Blanchard first introduced the term 'situational leadership' in 1967. For the scholars, situational leadership comprises four distinct leadership styles: telling, selling, participating and delegating. This leadership style is characterized by:

1. The ability of the leader to adjust effective leadership style with the maturity level of his subordinates and
2. The ability to address both hierarchical and collegial relationships (Hoy & Miskel, 1991).

Situational leadership does not deal with the personality, but rather with the behaviour of the individuals or the groups.

Instructional Leadership

Research indicates that the key person for providing instructional leadership in schools is the principal (Brookover, 1979; Edmonds, 1979). The essential aim of instructional leadership is to improve education by strengthening teachers' skills, curriculum integration, organizational structures improvement, and parents' and community members' involvement.

The main characteristics of instructional leaders are as follows:

1. They are known as culture builders because they infuse high expectations and standards for students and teachers (Barth, 1990).
2. They are goal-oriented with clear objectives for the schools and towards students' achievement).
3. They use strategies for coordination and aligning with the school's mission and vision.
4. They lead and manage the school both at the same time.

In addition, according to the National Association of Secondary School Principals' Handbook on Effective Instructional Leadership (1984), there are four main traits of an effective instructional leader. He/she:

1. Holds high expectations for teachers and staff.
2. Spends most times of his/her day working with other teachers in improving instructional materials.
3. Works in identifying and analysing instructional problems.
4. Is involved in influencing school effectiveness.

Transformational Leadership

James McGregor Burns first proposed transformational leadership in 1978. Most leadership models have been structured around personality traits, situational constraints and functional roles of the leaders (Hackman & Johnson, 1991) but not the transformational leadership.

Hackman and Johnson (1991) identify five personal qualities that transformational leaders should possess:

1. Creativity: Creativity can be a tool for improving problem-solving and motivating actions.

2. Interactive: Interactive leaders provide better direction.
3. Vision: "Transformational leaders communicate a vision to their followers" (p. 65). However, according to Bennis and Nanus (1985), these leaders must both verbalize avision and prepare an action plan.
4. Empowerment: This refers to the ability to "translate intention into reality and sustain it for the followers" (Bennis & Nanus, 1985:80).
5. Passion: The transformational leader is passionate about his or her commitment to the task and the staff alike. Bennis and Nanus expand this when they state that, "like explorers and artists, leaders seem to focus their attention on a limited field, their task being to forget personal problems, to lose their sense of time, to feel competent and in control" (p. 76).

According to Blanchard and Peale (1988), one significant personality trait omitted by Hackman and Johnson (1991) is a high ethical standard. They believe that a leader with high ethical standards can do the right thing and that ethics must be present in the decision-making process. A transformational leader is committed to responding ethically to various situations.

Thus, transformational leadership model emphasizes participative decision-making. This type of leader is people-oriented rather than task- and performance-oriented provides the opportunity for empowerment, and emphasizes on collegiality. The transformational leader is an encourager rather than an autocrat and a facilitator rather than a 'know-it-all.

Servant Leadership

Following Greenleaf (1977), servant leadership theory states that a person can be both a leader and a servant. This model of leadership emphasizes that leadership can be understood in terms of the development of consciousness and value and that leadership styles cannot be separated from followership styles.

Hall and Thompson (1980) identify seven levels of leadership-followership style characterized by the attitudes, values and skills of the leaders and the followers are depicted in Table 2.1.

The levels presented are hierarchically based on skill development. The higher the level, the more effective the leader becomes. The primary focus of this model is the servant first. It starts with a feeling that people want to serve. Then through some choices, the person aspires to become a leader.

Table 2.1. Seven levels of leadership-followership style

Level	Style	Attributes
1	*The Alienated person*	Alienated people exercise the most primitive type of leadership. This level corresponds to McGregor's Theory X (1960), which states that people hate to work and, therefore, must be threatened with punishment to get the job done. The followers see themselves as victims of power; they become fearful and alienate themselves from the leader.
2	*The Preservative person*	Preservative leaders become paternal in their behaviours; survival still dominates but the leaders do not feel as alienated. The followers at this level remain dependent but see their leader more positively. The followers still obey their leader but experience a variety of less demeaning behaviours.
3	*The Organization person*	The organization person, both leader and follower, is loyal to the bureaucracy. Productivity and competency are essential. The leader listens to the followers but supports only those ideas that benefit the organization
4	*The Communal person*	The communal leader, as well as the follower, become clarifiers, supporters and listeners. The leadership style is laissez-faire. Consequently, nothing gets done.
5	*The Independent person*	The independent person, both leader and follower, begins to experience his or her creativity and authority. The leader at this level is democratic, has empathy, is enthusiastic and visionary, listens to the followers and shows care and concern.
6	*The Creator person*	The creator person's leadership is based on the theory of peer interdependence. Leadership at this level develops both interpersonal and systems skills. This level marks the transition into a new phase of consciousness in which the leader examines the part in relation to the whole. At this level, leadership emphasizes the efficiency and productivity of the institution as well as the quality of human interaction within the organization.
7	*The Person as Prophet*	This level of leadership is not found in the working order of leadership. Level 7's leadership exists only as a prophet who assists the leader in becoming aware of the most global vision.

Source: Hall and Thompson (1980).

Strategic Leadership Characteristics

This subsection addresses strategic leadership style and its characteristics. Strategic leadership practices are the independent variable of this study. Thus, detailed explanation regarding strategic leadership will better assist the understanding of the concept of the independent variable under study. The discussion starts with strategic leadership in general and narrows down to the strategic leadership framework by Davies and Davies (2004) that is used as the intended independent variable.

Research in the field of strategic leadership naturally progresses towards tabulating strategic leader competencies. Starting from the 1980s, social science researchers began to study leadership with more attention to the leadership of organizations rather than conventional leadership attributes. Various styles of leadership such as transformational leadership, visionary leadership, and charismatic leadership terms have emerged, giving rise to the notion of strategic leadership.

Cheng (2000) defines strategic leadership as "determining where an organization was heading and how to get there". The process includes strategic and 'long-range' planning. Bola and Hooijberg (2000) list three factors of a strategic leader in their view relating to the essence of strategic leadership:

1. Creating and maintaining absorptive capacity (the ability to learn by acknowledging new information, processing it and applying it).
2. Creating and maintaining adaptive capacity (the ability to change based on a situation).
3. Obtaining managerial wisdom (consisting discernment and intuition).

According to Bolt (1996), are three dimensions of a leader: business, leadership, and personal effectiveness. The business aspect focuses on executive development including creating new forms of organizations, leading change and directing the organization.

Covey (1996) states that strategic leaders have three primary functions: path finding, aligning and empowering. Path finding compromises the process of aligning the organization's value with the company's vision and mission. Aligning involves the process of ensuring the organizational structure, systems and operational procedures in-line with the organization's mission and vision. Empowering ignites the talent, ingenuity and creativity of the followers to accomplish the mission.

Quong and Walker (2010) emphasize seven principles a strategic leader should have:

1. Future-oriented and have future strategy (Davies & Ellison, 2003)
2. Evidence-based and research led (Groundwater-Smith, 2000; Davies & Ellison 2003)
3. Get things done (Robinson, 2007; Elmore, 2002)
4. Open new horizons.
5. Fit to lead (Elmore, 2002)
6. Make good partners (Robinson, 2007)
7. Do the 'next' right thing (Ramsey, 2003)

On the other hand, Weick (2001) lists only two attributes of strategic leaders:

1. Improvisation (making something new or good from experience, practice and knowledge)
2. Lightness (the ability to drop anything that is no longer useful).

As explained above, there has been various definitions and characterization of strategic leadership. Some authors look at it from the individual characteristics of a leader's point of view, and others define strategic elements in the organization. For the purpose of this research, the strategic leadership concept by Davies (2006) and Davies and Davies (2004; 2009) are applied. Davies (2006) and Davies and Davies (2004; 2009) combined five individual characteristics and four organizational capabilities for a strategic leader. They highlight nine characteristics of a strategic leader:

1. <u>Restlessness</u> - 'creative tension' which emerges from seeing clearly where one wishes to be, one's vision, and facing the truth about one's current reality (Senge, 1990).
2. <u>Absorptive</u> - the ability to absorb new information, assimilate it and learn from it and most importantly, apply it to new ends (Cohen & Levinthal, 1990).
3. <u>Adaptive</u> - the ability to change (Black & Bola, 1996; Hambrick, 1989).
4. <u>Wisdom</u> – the capacity to take the right action at the right time (Davies & Davies, 2004).

5. Strategic orientation – the ability to consider both long-term futures (Stacey, 1992; Boisot, 1995; Beare, 2001; Adair, 2002), seeing the bigger picture, as well as understanding the current contextual setting of the organization (Davies & Davies, 2004).

6. Strategic translation – the need to translate strategy into action by converting it into operational terms (Davies & Davies, 2004).

7. Strategic alignment - This ability of aligning individuals, or the school as a whole, to a future organizational state or position (Gioia & Thomas, 1996; Gratton, 2000; Davies, 2003).

8. Strategic intervention - the key moment for strategic change in organizations (Burgleman & Grove, 1996).

9. Strategic competence - the ability to develop strategic capabilities (Prahalad & Hamel, 1990).

Instruments Measuring Leadership

This subsection briefly explains some commonly used instruments measuring leadership styles, which are Leadership Skills Inventory (LSI), Least Preferred Co-worker (LPC), Leader-Member Exchange (LMX-7) and Multifactor Leadership Questionnaire (MLQ).

Leadership Skills Inventory (LSI)

LSI uses 'self' and 'other' method of measuring leadership skills of a person. If the instrument demonstrates congruent validity, then the "measured" 'self' has the leadership competencies (Anderson & Wanberg, 1991). LSI is a 125 item Likert-style instrument with nine attributes of leadership including fundamentals of leadership, written communication, speech communication skills, values' clarification, decision-making skills, group dynamic skills, problem-solving skills, personal development skills, and planning skills.

LSI demonstrates empirical support of content and constructs validity (Edmunds, 1998). A uni-dimensional model (with loading ranges from .636 to .876) and correlation among the attributes between .295 to .761, $p < .01$ is concluded. A high score is a sign of a leader prioritizing on good personal relations while a low score is an indication that the emphasis is more on productivity and tasks. Internal reliability is reported at alpha .64 and average internal consistency of coefficients of .88 (Rice, 1978).

Least Preferred Co-worker (LPC)

The assumption of this model is leadership style is fixed but in a different situation, task structure and different hierarchical position, it requires certain style of leadership. The aim is to match leadership style to the situation (Fielder cited in Robbins et al., 1994). The instrument comprises 188-point bipolar adjective scales. Instead of asking about the leader or the subordinate, it asks the leader about the personnel he/she has found it most difficult to work with (they describe their 'least preferred co-worker'). A high score indicates that the leader stresses on good personal relations while a low score reflects an emphasis on an official relationship only. Reliability is at alpha .64 and the average internal consistency of coefficients of .88 (Rice, 1978).

Leader-MemberExchange (LMX-7)

LMX measures the dyadic relationship between an individual member and his/her supervisor, and describes reciprocal fulfilment of expectations (Graen et al., 1982). LMX is positively related to performance and satisfaction (Graen et al., 1982), locus of control and time-based pressure (Kinicki & Vecchio, 1994), delegation (Schriesheim et al., 1998), job attitudes and performance evaluations (Dienesch & Liden, 1986), and commitment and citizenship behaviour. The LMX-7 instrument contains seven items that measure the quality of exchange between leader and subordinate and is completed by the subordinates. In the context of education, LMX7 can be used to examine the quality of social relationships perceived by teachers among themselves and their superior. However, LMX is more useful in a hierarchical organization with managers and supervisors, rather than organizations with a flat structure.

Multifactor Leadership Questionnaire (MLQ)

The MLQ comprises subscales and uses a 5-pointLikert-type scale. The MLQ measures characteristics of leaders and the effects on the followers, from the perspective of the followers (Shamir et al., 1998). It measures transactional, transformational and *laissez-faire* leadership style of a leader. It is broadly applicable to a wide range of organizations and at any level of the organization where there is a superior-subordinate relationship. The MLQ is the most frequently used questionnaire (Bass & Avolio, 1985).

Previous Studies on Leadership

Various studies have been carried out on leadership. Most of the studies employed quantitative research design using purposive and random sampling technique. Majority of them examined subordinates' views towards their leaders. One paper by Price (2008) investigates the different leadership styles with teachers' motivation. It is found that autocratic leadership has a significant negative relationship on teachers' motivation and democratic leadership has a positive significant on teachers' motivation, while a *laissez-faire* leadership style has no relationship on teachers' motivation.

Many of the studies discussed leadership characteristics of a leader (e.g. Kalargyrou, 2012; Pisapia & Ying, 2011; Coffin, 2008). Only a few studies have investigated strategic leadership. Examples of the studies are Adelakun (2015), Ali (2013), William and Johnson (2013), Nazifah (2013) and Hairuddin (2012).

Adelakun (2015), Ali (2013), Hairuddin (2012) and Nazifah (2012) use the same strategic leadership characteristics by Davies and Davies (2004, 2006, 2009) to explore the strategic leadership practices of school principals. Adelakun (2015) and Ali (2013) further the study by exploring the relationship between strategic leadership and teachers' self-efficacy. It can be clearly seen that research in strategic leadership has received little attention. Thus, there is still avast opportunity to explore strategic leadership.

Leadership from the Islamic Perspective

Islam views leadership as a responsibility and as part of worshipping Allah (S.W.T). Leadership in Islam is not only aimed at serving members of the organization, but the most important goal is to direct and guide people to what is good in this world and the Hereafter.

Early Muslim scholars used the *wilaya* to represent leadership. *Wilaya* is defined as "maintaining the religion of the people such that if it is lost, they will be the losers, and maintaining a life that will assist people to understand their religion" (Ibn Taymiya, 1992: 11).

Another important term in Islamic leadership is *Imamah*. Al-Mawardi (1983) uses the word *Imamah* to describe leadership in the context of "guarding of the religion and life" (Basbous 1988:47; Al-Wakil 1988:22). Ali (1985) explains that *Imam* means the "leader in religion or leader in congregational prayer or model, pattern, and example." (p. 50). Thus, *imamah* is leadership.

Murad Khurram defines leadership as "the ability to see beyond assumed boundaries and to come up with solutions or paths that few can visualize. The leader must then project this vision for everyone to see and pursue" (quoted in Beekun & Badawi, 1999: 5- 6) which relates the leadership with vision.

Many scholars instill the element of influence in the definition of leadership. For example, Basbous (1988) defines leadership as the "art of influencing and directing others towards a common objective in a way that leaders will gain their members' trust, respect, cooperation and sincere obedience". Similarly, Beekunand Badawi (1999) define leadership as "the process of directing and influencing organization members so that they will take ownership of organizational activities and programmes".

In Islam, leadership is about guiding people to what is good in this world and the Hereafter. Thus, leadership does not only deal with an organization in the context of its daily work, but also must be connected to the religion's objectives. Specifically, leadership has a connection with religion and the Creator. The next section looks at five roles of educational leadership in Islam.

The Visionary Educational Leader

A Muslim leader is a forward-looking person with a vision of the future rather than just the daily objectives of the organization. The clear vision guides him towards the achievement of the objectives by following the right way and method. The leader's view will clarify why one is here, how and what one is doing and what one will be doing in the future. Leaders have to transform this clear vision to the members of the organization.

Allah (S.W.T) asked the Prophet (P.B.U.H.) and his companions to be patient and not to fight with their oppressors because the final vision had yet to be reached. Allah (S.W.T) said in the Qur'an, "Hast thou not turned thy thought to those who were told to hold back their hands (from fight) but establish regular prayers and spend in regular Zakah..."(Qur'an 4:77).

The Servant Leader

Serving one's people is one of the primary roles of a Muslim leader. Educational leadership in this context is not a matter of privilege or position but rather a vast responsibility. Educational leaders need to therefore, feel that they are the servants of their followers. This feeling will help leaders to make great efforts towards protecting the members of the organization and do whatever is necessary to achieve its objectives.

The Prophet (P.B.U.H.) said, "A ruler who has been entrusted with the affairs of the Muslims but makes no endeavour (for the material and moral upliftment) and is not sincerely concerned (for their welfare) will not enter Paradise along with them." (Muslim, n.d. Vol. 1, ch. 44, hadith No. 264, p. 82).

The Leader as a Guide

A Muslim leader is concerned about his followers' well being. His concern is related to directing the members towards understanding the vision of the organization and how they are going to achieve success in their duties in the best manner.

Allah (S.W.T) said in the Qur'an, "And We made them leaders, guiding (men) by Our command, and We inspired them to do good deeds, to establish regular prayers and to give Zakah and they constantly served Us (and Us only)" (Qur'an 21:73).

The Influential Leader

A Muslim leader's job is not only to serve and guide people but also to bring changes for the betterment of their lives. A prominent leader is connected with changes from the wrong to the right. By influencing the followers, leaders will be able to transform their spirit, knowledge and experience to everybody in the organization. However, this will not be achieved unless leaders are good models and examples for their followers. The Prophet (P.B.U.H.) was very successful in influencing people and guiding them to the new religion - beginning with his wife Khadija (R.A), his close companion Abu Bakr al-Siddiq (R.A) and later, all other companions (Abdul-Wahhab, 1997:97).

The Educative Leader

An educational leader needs to be concerned with the enhancement of the potentials and capabilities of all members: spiritually, mentally, intellectually, psychologically, socially and professionally. The Prophet (p.b.u.h.) used to teach his companions in different ways, especially when somebody was given a position involving leadership. It had been reported that when Prophet

Muhammad (p.b.u.h.) appointed Ali Ibn Abi Talib (r.a.) as a judge in Yemen, he was concerned that he had no experience in the field. Regarding this incident, Ali (r.a.) said:, "the Prophet (p.b.u.h.) sent me to Yemen as a judge. I said, Oh! Messenger of Allah! I am a youth, how could you send me to a people who are far advanced in years than me. The Prophet prayed for me, and said: "If two adversaries approach you; (for fair judgement) and you hear the claim of one, do not judge until you have heard from the other, for this is to decide the case"(al-Baihaqi n.d., Vol.10, Kitab A'dab al- Qadi, p. 86). It is clear here that Prophet Muhammad (p.b.u.h.) had taught Ali (r.a.) the central and most general rule to be practised by a judge. Muslim leaders, therefore, should follow such examples and train their followers how to do the assigned jobs. By doing this, members will be more confident in tackling their duties and, as a result, they will be more professional in their concerned fields.

CHAPTER THREE

ORGANIZATIONAL BUREAUCRACY

INTRODUCTION

This chapter deals with organizational bureaucracy. It begins by discussing the concept of organizational bureaucracy, and then highlights several instruments used to measure organizational bureaucracy. Finally, a brief review of previous studies on organizational bureaucracy is presented.

THE CONCEPT OF ORGANIZATIONAL BUREAUCRACY

The concept of bureaucracy was introduced by Max Weber (Etzioni, 1961). According to Weber, there are seven organizational attributes that when present, constitute the bureaucratic form of organization:

1. A continuous body of official functions bound by rules.
2. A specific sphere of competence.
3. The principle of hierarchy.
4. Rules that regulate the conduct of an office.
5. Complete separationof members of the administrative staff from ownership of the means of production or administration.
6. Organizational resources that is free of any outside control and absence of any position monopoly by any incumbent.
7. Formulation and recording of administrative acts, decisions, and any rules in writing (pp. 53-54).

Jones (2004) defines bureaucracy as a form of organizational structure in which people are held accountable for their actions and are required to act by specified rules and standard operating procedures. Robbins (1998) asserts that bureaucracy relies on standardized work processes for coordination and control, and characterized by:

1. Highly routine operating tasks achieved through specialization
2. Very formalized rules and regulations
3. Tasks are grouped into functional departments
4. Centralized authority
5. Narrow spans of control
6. Decision-making that follows the chain of command

Bureaucracy is a powerful institution that significantly enhances potential capacities because of the neutral instruments of rational administration on a large scale (Motala & Pampallis, 2001). The primary strength of bureaucracy is the ability to perform standardized activities in an efficient manner. Jones (2004) argues that bureaucracy lays out the basis for designing an organizational hierarchy and increases the efficiency of those interactions. The above opinions are in line with Shafritz and Ott (2001) who advocate bureaucracy as the only form of guidelines that help a company to employ large numbers of people and yet serve to maintain accountability for the work they do.

In schools, bureaucracy can act as a practical tool in management (Smith and Meier, 1994, 1995). It has a positive impact when problems exist as the absence of administrators would require teachers to be responsible, forcing them to spend more time on administrative matters rather than teaching. Reducing bureaucracy in schools could probably lead to a decrease in performance, as fewer experts are available to address administrative matters.

Despite its strengths, bureaucracy suffers from a number of weaknesses. Robbins (1998) highlights two weaknesses:

1. Specialization creates sub-unit conflicts. As a result functional unit goals are given more attention than the overall goal of the organization.
2. Obsessive concern with following the rules, resulting in no room for modification.

Jones (2004) too acknowledges two major problems that emerge with bureaucracy:

1. Over time, managers fail to control the expansion of the organizational hierarchy. Thus, the organization becomes tall and centralized. Aspects such as decision-making begin to slow down; the organization begins to be static and bureaucratic costs increases.
2. Organizational members become individualistic because their chief goal is to follow rules and procedures and obey authority.

In addition to these weaknesses, Hellriegel et al. (2001) identify five drawbacks of bureaucratic management. A system with rigid rules leaves little room for individual freedom and creativity. This rigidity may promote negative office values such as low motivation and high turnover among best employees. Managers in a bureaucratic organization may prefer expanding their authority rather than dealing with issues of employee productivity. Furthermore, the organization is prone to slow decision-making, is incompatible with changing technology and has conflicting professional values. In a school environment, Chubb and Moe (1990) found that centralized bureaucracies limit teachers' creativity to propose and implement innovative solutions to educational problems. As a result, public schools tend to perform poorly.

INSTRUMENTS USED TO MEASURE ORGANIZATIONAL BUREAUCRACY

Two instruments are commonly used to measure bureaucracy: Hall (1961), and Hoy and Sweetland (2001). Most bureaucracy research makes use of Hall's bureaucracy instrument.

Organizational Inventory

Hall (1961) was the first to quantify the degree of bureaucratization in organizations with six dimensions of bureaucracy: hierarchy of authority, division of labour, rules and regulations, procedural specifications, impersonality and technical competence, all of which are placed under Organizational Inventory. Organizational Inventory has 62 items. All dimensions have ten items except for hierarchy of authority, which has 12 items. Hall's (1961) instrument has been modified by many researchers such as MacKay (1964), Robinson (1966), Kolesar (1967), Punch (1967), Anderson (1970), Isherwood (1971), and Sousa (1980). This research uses the instrument modified by Yucel (1999). To develop his instrument, Yucel (1999) mapped all the above researchers' work and came up with his own. The reliability of his constructs ranges from .64 to .82.

Enabling School Structure

Enabling School Structure (ESS) is an instrument developed by Hoy and Sweetland (2001) based on a dichotomous measure whether the organizational bureaucracy hinders or enables school functionality. The instrument only considers two out of six Weber's Bureaucracy dimensions, i.e. hierarchy of authority and rules and regulations.

The ESS Form is a 12-item Likert-type scale. It measures the degree to which school structure is enabling; the higher the score, the more enabling the school structure, and vice versa. The reliability of the scale is high, .90 or greater (Hoy & Sweetland, 2001). The construct validity has been strongly supported by some studies (Hoy & Sweetland, 2000, Hoy & Sweetland, 2001).

PREVIOUS STUDIES ON ORGANIZATIONAL BUREAUCRACY

Majority of the studies on organizational bureaucracy employed a quantitative approach (e.g. Lennon, 2009; Naido, 2008; Robinson, 2004). They either use longitudinal data or survey method with random sampling technique. The majority of the research populations were teachers and students. However, there is one study (Pandey, 2007) that used managers as the population.

A review of these studies indicates inconsistent findings in terms of the effects of bureaucracy on students' performance. Meier et al. (2000), for instance, found that bureaucracy has little influence on students' performance. However, bureaucratic growth is the result of poor students' performance. Meanwhile, Smith and Lariner (2004) prove that bureaucracy mediates the measures of school performance. Smith and Lariner (2004) claim that bureaucracies are successful at fulfilling secondary goals such as attendance rates and graduation rates. Lennon's (2009) findings are parallel to Smith and Lariner's (2004) whereby the academic achievement of students, although not an independent construct, is influenced by all of the dimensions of climate and the bureaucratic structure of the school. However, Lennon (2009) did not specify in which direction bureaucracy influences school performance. Another research that has the same paradigm was by Bohte (2001). Bohte (2001) reveals that negative relationships exist between bureaucracy and students' performance.

Bureaucracy also impacts the professional practice of teachers (Volk, 2012), and budgeting process (Robinson, 2004), and has a negative effect on organizational effectiveness (Pandey & Kinsley, 2007). Current literature has outlined mixed reviews relating to bureaucracy and school performance.

CHAPTER FOUR

IN-SERVICE TRAINING EFFECTIVENESS

INTRODUCTION

This chapter is concerned with Continuous Professional Development (CPD). It begins by describing the characteristics of CPD, followed by a discussion on the instruments used to evaluate CPD. The chapter ends with a brief review of previous studies on CPD.

IN-SERVICE TRAINING (IST): THE IMPORTANCE OF CONTINUOUS PROFESSIONAL DEVELOPMENT (CPD)

Continuous Professional Development (CPD) is a multidimensional process that encompasses all aspects of training, from the readiness activities, practice, and coaching through follow-up and support activities (Guskey & Sparks, 1991). According to Day (1999:5) "CPD encompasses all natural learning experiences and those conscious and planned activities, which are intended to be of direct or indirect benefit to the individual, group or school".

Wood et al. (1981) identify five levels of CPD training for teachers:

- Level 1: Readiness - The organizers identify the problem and the desired change and choose appropriate programmes and processes. Participants understand and are committed to changing the behaviour of professionals.

- Level 2: Planning - This step is important to ensure that the goals outlined are more specific, the need to have studied programmes, planned programme activities, identify resources to be used and the level of training design and implementation.
- Level 3: Training - When the plan is implemented, content, skills and attitudes that are needed to change professional behaviour are learned.
- Level 4: Implementation - The stage where what has been learned in the training is carried out. Thus, an environment that encourages 'transition' from what they have learned during the training programme into the daily activities in the workplace is necessary.
- Level 5: Retention - (maintenance) - The new behaviour is not eternal even though it has been implemented. This ensures continuous detection by the school to determine whether the behaviouris still practised and accomplishes goals.

CPD is acknowledged as one of the important elements in improving teaching and learning activities (Hargreaves, 1994; Harland & Kinder, 1997; Craft, 2000). It includes staff development and improving teaching and learning activities that contribute to school effectiveness (Maden & Hillman, 1996; Gray, 2000; OFSTED, 2000). It also improves learning outcomes (Bennett et al., 2010).

The most important stage in CPD is the retention or effective evaluation. This stage is the phase where appropriate professional development is provided to achieve particular professional needs (Garret, 2001). This 'fit' between the developmental needs and professional teacher needs is important, and has a positive impact on the school and classroom levels (Hopkins & Harris, 2001).

CPD can be evaluated at each level. To minimize bias in evaluating CPD, data need to be collected from all stakeholders rather than just one group of stakeholder. Further, a variety of research method should be used (Smith, 2002), and continuous feedback should be provided.

IN-SERVICE TRAINING (IST) EVALUATION INSTRUMENTS

In general, there are two common tools used to evaluate training programmes: the Kirkpatrick Evaluation Model, and the Guskey 5-Level of Professional Development Evaluation. The first evaluation model is mostly used worldwide, but the second model emphasizes evaluation model in the education field.

The Kirkpatrick Evaluation Model

The Kirkpatrick evaluation model, which was updated in 1975 and 1994, comprises four levels of evaluation. The four levels are reaction, learning, behaviour and results, as described below.

- Level 1: Reaction. This level measures how the trainees (the people being trained), reacted to the training including the instructor, the topic, the materials, the presentation and the venue. It is important to measure reactions because it helps to understand how well the training is received by the audience. It also helps in improving the training for future trainees, including identifying important areas or topics that are missing from the training.
- Level 2: Learning. Level 2 measures what the trainees have learned. How much has their knowledge increased as a result of the training? Learning can be measured in different ways depending on the programme objectives, and depending on which learning elements to measure, i.e. changes to knowledge, skills, or attitude.
- Level 3: Behaviour. At this level, the evaluation is on the change of behaviour, based on the training received. Specifically, this looks at how trainees apply the information. However, just because the behaviour has not changed, it does not mean that trainees have not learned anything.
- Level 4: Results. At this level, the analyses of the final results come into the picture. This includes outcomes of the organization.

The Guskey 5-Level of Professional Development Evaluation

Guskey (2000a) identifies five levels at which the impact of CPD can be evaluated. These are:

1. Participants' reactions
2. Participants' learning
3. Organizational support and change
4. Participants'use of new knowledge and skills
5. Students' learning outcomes

Each of the levels is explained below.

- Level 1: Participants' Reactions.
  Questions addressed at Level 1 will include whether the participants enjoyed the event, thought it was useful, addressed their needs, was well-presented and well organized, for example. Three main types of questions can be answered using this approach: content questions, process questions and context questions (Guskey, 2000a).

- Level 2: Participants' learning from CPD.
  Level 2 comprises participants' learning from CPD. There are several types of learning: cognitive, affective or behavioural, that can result from CPD. These different types of knowledge are acquired and modified in different ways, thus probably requiring different methods of evaluation. As well as specific knowledge and skills, and affective outcomes, CPD may result in renewed commitment of teachers as change agents and renewed or extended moral purpose.

- Level 3: Organizational Support and Change.
  CPD activities have been found to transfer more easily into changed behaviours and teaching practices if there is a good fit with individuals' professional and personal values and if professional development approaches already exist in the organization (Knight, 2002). As well as being important in leading to the success of CPD programmes, organizational change can often be a prime goal of CPD programmes. Therefore, organizational level outcomes and support are important parts of CPD evaluation since they would have an impact on motivation on the one hand and sustainability of change on the other.

- Level 4: Participants' Use of New Knowledge and Skills.
  Evaluation of this level will have to take place after a reasonable time, the length of which will depend on the complexity of the knowledge or skills to be acquired and the amount of time participants require to develop and practice these skills (Guskey, 2000a).

- Level 5: Student Outcomes.
  This is the one least likely to be measured in evaluations at present, but also the one that is most important because it assesses the impact on student learning. Student learning can be defined and measured in some ways. The first distinction is between cognitive outcomes such as mathematical attainment and non-cognitive outcomes such as attitudes to school and engagement in learning. Each requires different methods to determine programme effects (Guskey, 2000a).

Guskey (2000a) sees CPD impact as linear across these levels. This means that impact at one level is only possible if the impact has taken place at previous levels and that impact at a certain level does not imply impact at the subsequent level. The desirable result is at level 5, the impact on students' learning. It accommodates measuring learning in terms of knowledge, skills, attitudes, and values, social or emotional development. Guskey's evaluation model does not intend to be able to explain the impact, or lack of it, at various levels.

PREVIOUS STUDIES ON CPD

Most research on CPD employed mixed method design (e.g. Kennedy, 2011; Pedder et al., 2010), and many of them are in the education field (e.g. Pedder & Opfer, 2010; Waters and Wall, 2008). However, research in CPD has discovered an enormous mismatch between training and the actual needs of the recipients. This mismatch may be attributed to issues related to the planning and organization of CPD. According to Pedder and Opfer (2010), there is a lack of strategic planning on CPD to balance between individual and organizational learning needs and national policy priorities. In addition, organizational choices in schools do not always support or help to develop effective CPD planning and provision. Furthermore, processes for evaluating the effectiveness of CPD tend to be developed without reference to organizational goals.

The mismatch clearly disturbs the cycle of CPD and most importantly affects the students' performances. According to Harris et al. (2010), the impact of CPD on student learning remains significantly under-evaluated. Guskey (1994) supports the view by pointing out three major weaknesses in evaluative practice:

1. The evaluation may often amount to no more than documentation of activities completed over a period of time.
2. Evaluation often does not go deeply enough, being limited to 'happiness questionnaires' after the event.
3. Evaluation is often too brief. Just as professional development should be anon-going process, so should its evaluation.

CHAPTER FIVE

STUDENTS' ASPIRATION OUTCOMES

INTRODUCTION

This chapter discusses students' aspiration outcomes as the independent variable in this research. The discussion starts with the general concept of students' educational aspirations, students' aspirations as the organizational goals and past research regarding students' aspirations.

THE CONCEPT OF STUDENTS' EDUCATIONAL ASPIRATIONS

The term 'aspiration' lends itself to a variety of definitions and interpretations. Does it refer to goals, expectations, or dreams? Should aspirations be viewed from a short term or long term perspective (or both)? In general, aspirations are a strong desire for some object or condition, but the general understanding of the term 'aspiration' is not quite right. Reissman (1953) states that"... aspirations refer to a future time period and consequently there often is no opportunity to check upon the reliability of a subject's aspirations" (p. 233). He indicates that most research involving college students' aspirations during the 1950s revealed what was expected, "...that success leads to the raising of the level of aspirations and failure to a lowering of that level" (Reissmann, 1953; p. 234).

Flouri (2006) argues that the concept of 'aspiration' is often confounded with parents' expectations on their children's educational achievements. It is also associated with various desires and ambitions held by young people about

40

their future; these beliefs can be concrete or vague, but they are individual to the person.

An aspiration is a "non-intellectual" factor in academic achievement (Worrell, 1959). It has two distinctive aspects, i.e. future-oriented and motivators. They can only be achieved at some future time and they are goals that are related to the investment of time, effort or money (Sherwood, 1989). In the words of Hurlock (1967), aspiration means, "a longing for what is above one's achieved level with advancement on its end. In other words, aspiration means the goal individual sets for himself in a task, which has intense personal significance for him and in which he, is ego-involved".

Based on the above discussion, it can be concluded that students' aspiration by definition is the visions of the students for their future in the educational context.

STUDENTS' ASPIRATION OUTCOMES IN THE MALAYSIAN EDUCATION DEVELOPMENT PLAN (2013-2025)

Students' aspiration outcomes in the Malaysian Education Development Plan (2013-2025) are treated as the ultimate goals of the plan, besides the system aspirations. The outcomes are categorized into six elements: knowledge, thinking skills, leadership skills, bilingual proficiency, ethics and spirituality and national identity. All six students' aspiration outcomes constructs are explained in Table 5.1.

Table 5.1 Conceptual Definitions of Students' Aspiration Outcomes

Variables	Constructs	Definition
	Knowledge	Full literacy and numeracy, mastering core subjects (i.e. Mathematics and Science), informed by a rounded general knowledge of Malaysia, Asia, and the world and develop their knowledge and skills in other areas (i.e. arts, music, and sports).
	Thinking Skills	Mastering range of important cognitive skills (i.e. critical thinking, reasoning, creative thinking, and innovation).
	Leadership Skills	Reaching full potential by creating formal and informal opportunities for students to work in teams, and to take on leadership roles.
Students' Aspiration Outcomes	*Bilingual Proficiency*	Able to work in both Bahasa Malaysia and English language environment.
	Ethics & Spirituality	Inculcating strong ethics and spirituality to prepare the students to rise to the challenges they will inevitably face in adult life, resolve conflicts peacefully, to employ sound judgment and principles during critical moments, and to have the courage to do what is right.
	National Identity	Every child will proudly identify as Malaysian, irrespective of ethnicity, religion or socio-economic status. Achieving this patriotism requires that every child understand the country's history and shares common aspirations for the future.

Source: MOEM (2013)

PREVIOUS STUDIES ON STUDENTS' ASPIRATIONS

Research on aspirations had started as early as in 1931 when Dembo (1976) discovered the concept of "level of aspiration" while doing an experiment to investigate anger. An unintended consequence of the analysis was that subjects formulated their own, medial aim when the original objective was too difficult to attain. This transitional goal is called "momentary level of aspiration" (Gardiner, 1940). The level of aspiration refers to the subsequent level of performance, which an individual anticipates achieving following the performance on a task (Worell, 1959).

According to Bayton (1943), there are at least three levels of aspiration available to the individual:

1. The maximum level
2. The minimum level
3. The actual level

The maximum level represents the ultimate ability. The minimum level is the score below which the individual is confident he will not fall, whereas the actual level of aspiration is the score that the subject expects to make on the next trial. From then on, research on aspirations concentrated on contributory factors such as academic achievement, types of education, gender, parental involvement and socio-economic status. Concerning academic achievement, Astone and McLanahan (1991) reveal that"...high aspirations are a critical factor predicting educational achievement" (p. 310). Other findings are consistent with studies by Astone and McLanahan (1991), Jencks et al. (1983) and Hanson (1994). Aspirations are also closely related to the types of education received by students. Students exposed to a particular type of education may have different levels of aspirations to those not exposed to that type of education (Harbison, 1991).

Many research relating gender to students' aspirations have found a significant relationship between the two variables. Male undergraduate students have a higher level of aspiration than female undergraduate students in a study by Rahman and Goswami (2013). Williams (1972) asserts that women's achievements when translated into aspirations are lower than men. However, according to Schoon et al. (2007), women consistently have higher aspirations than men. This gender differential pattern is especially apparent in the school and academic environment and has been observed throughout the educational lifecycle: in elementary school, in children's aspirations for college attendance (Wylie, 1963), high school students' levels of occupational ambition (Marini & Greenberger, 1978), college students' predictions of course grades (Vaughter et al., 1974), and graduate students' aspirations for a university versus a junior college teaching career (Feldman, 1974).

Parental involvement may also influence students' aspirations. Buchmann and Dalton (2002) argue that parental involvement in schooling influences aspirations but not achievement. However, students who had career aspirations were more likely to have family members as role models (Strand & Winston, 2008). Social class has been found to be important in aspirations (Kintrea, 2009). Socially disadvantaged groups such as teenage parents have lower aspirations for themselves and their children (Gutman & Akerman (2008). Parents with fewer financial resources tend to hold lower aspirations for their children, and young people from socially disadvantaged backgrounds tend to have lower aspirations than their more advantaged peers (Schoon, 2007). Sewell and Shah (1968) and Solarzano (1992) also note that "an important and consistent finding in the area of stratification research is that the children of higher social class origins are more likely to aspire to high educational and occupational goals than are the children of lower social class origins" (p. 191).

THE HYPOTHESIZED MODEL OF THE STUDY

Based on the methodological analysis of separate variables in the previous chapters, a conceptual framework is developed. The anchor of the framework is the Upper Echelons Theory (UET) that defines that top management act by their highly personalized interpretations of the situations and options they face, based on their experiences, personalities, and values translated into their behaviours to the extent, those actions impact the organization's performance. Most research using UET were done in the business field of the corporate world. Little knowledge has been contributed to the education field using this theory.

The independent variable of this study is strategic leadership, whereby the decision made by top management is based on the strategic choices they have. Research in leadership normally focuses on the characteristics of the leader or the leadership styles. However, less information is known about strategic leadership specifically in the school environment. No instruments were developed to measure strategic leadership practices compared to other leadership styles.

The independent variable involved is students' aspiration outcomes. According to the UET, strategic choices will influence organizational performance. Thus, in the context of this study, students' aspiration outcomes are used to benchmark the Malaysian education system. This is based on the recently launched Malaysian Education Development Plan (2013-2025), which has students' aspiration outcomes as the ultimate goal of the success of the Malaysian education system. Research in students' aspiration outcomes, narrows the determinants influencing students' aspirations. No research has been conducted relating students' aspirations to other variables.

Two mediating variables are involved in the research, i.e. organizational bureaucracy and in-service training effectiveness. Both variables have mixed findings on students' performance. Based on previous research, the organizational bureaucracy has either negative influence or no influence on students' performance while in-service training effectiveness influences teachers' professionalism but the relationship between in-service training effectiveness and students' performance is under-evaluated. Combining the four variables together, the hypothesized model of the study is depicted in Figure 5.1.

Based on Figure 5.1, the research hypotheses are as follows:

H_1: The strategic leadership practices measurement model is valid and reliable.

H_2: The organizational bureaucracy measurement model is valid and reliable.

H_3: The in-service training effectiveness measurement model is valid and reliable.

H_4: The students' aspiration outcomes measurement model is valid and reliable.

H_5: There is a direct and significant relationship between strategic leadership practices and students' aspiration outcomes.

H_6 There is a direct and significant relationship between organizational bureaucracy and students' aspiration outcomes.

H_7: There is a direct and significantrelationship between in-service training effectiveness and students' aspiration outcomes.

H_8: Organizational bureaucracy mediates the relationship between strategic leadership practices and students' aspiration outcomes.

H_9: In-service training effectiveness mediates the relationship between strategic leadership practices and students' aspiration outcomes.

H_{10}: The revised hypothesized structural equation model is valid and reliable.

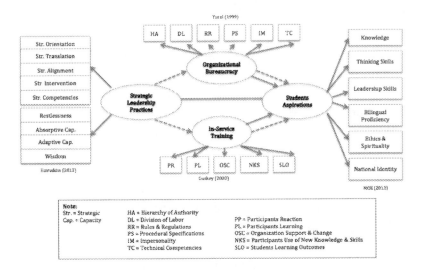

Sources: Hairuddin (2012), Yucel (1999), Guskey (2000a), Ministry of Education Malaysia (2013).

Figure 5.1 The Hypothesized Model of the Study

CHAPTER SIX

THE RESEARCH METHODS

RESEARCH DESIGN

This research employed a quantitative research design. The research design was chosen due to the nature of this research, which is for theory verification and to find answers to a phenomenon through empirical observation. Philips and Burbules (2000) categorize the nature of this research as post-positivism. According to them, post-positivism research requires the determination of effects or outcomes. Thus, the problems under study reflect the need to examine the causes that influence outcomes, which is exactly the aim of this research.

The selection of a quantitative design for this research is appropriate based on Muijs' (2004) contextualization. Muijs (2004) highlights four conditions whereby quantitative research design is appropriate:

1. When we want a quantitative answer
2. When numerical change can accurately be studied using quantitative method
3. To find out the state of something
4. Testing of hypotheses

The study utilized cross-sectional survey design. This design is normally used to measure current attitudes, beliefs, opinions or practices (Creswell, 2005). The means for data collection is to disseminate paper questionnaires to the sampled respondents. To ensure rigorousness of the survey findings, random sampling technique was used to confirm the representativeness of the population (Creswell, 2009; Keppel, 1991).

THE POPULATION

As briefly mentioned in Chapter 1, the population under study is the leadership group (*kumpulan kepimpinan*) in the vocational colleges throughout Malaysia. There are 80 vocational colleges altogether. Table 6.1 presents the distribution of the population by each state. In each college, there are several leadership posts held by the teachers. Specifically, the leadership posts are:

1. Directors
2. Deputy Directors
3. Head of Departments
4. Head of Units
5. Lab Heads

Table 6.1. The Population of the Leadership
Group in Vocational Colleges as of 2015

No	State	Number of Vocational Colleges	Number of Leadership Posts
1	Perlis	2	74
2	Kedah	5	169
3	Pulau Pinang	5	154
4	Perak	10	331
5	Selangor	8	246
6	Negeri Sembilan	6	193
7	Melaka	3	106
8	Johor	8	258
9	Pahang	8	247
10	Terenganu	4	139
11	Kelantan	5	170
12	Sabah	8	288
13	Sarawak	6	214
14	WP Kuala Lumpur	2	64
	TOTAL	*80*	*2649*

Source: Vocational and Technical Division, Ministry of Education Malaysia (2012)

Every vocational college participated in this study in some manner. Out of the 80 vocational colleges, 15 were pilot vocational colleges (*Kolej Vokasional Rintis*). The participants from the 15 pilot vocational colleges took part in the pilot study, and the rest of the participants became the respondents for the eventual data collection. The populations under study were 562 (pilot study) and 2,087 (this study), respectively.

SAMPLING

Two different sampling techniques were involved in this study. Convenience sampling technique was used for the pilot study, and stratified random sampling technique was used for the eventual study. For a given population, Krejcie and Morgan (1970) come up with a table for the proposed sample size. Table 6.2 draws the sample size from a given population.

Table 6.2 Determination of Sample Size from a Given Population

N	S	N	S	N	S	N	S	N	S
10	10	100	80	280	162	800	260	2800	338
15	14	110	86	290	165	850	265	3000	341
20	19	120	92	300	169	900	269	3500	346
25	24	130	97	320	175	950	274	4000	351
30	28	140	103	340	181	1000	278	4500	351
35	32	150	108	360	186	1100	285	5000	357
40	36	160	113	380	191	1200	291	6000	361
45	40	170	118	400	196	1300	297	7000	364
50	44	180	123	420	201	1400	302	8000	367
55	48	190	127	440	205	1500	306	9000	368
60	52	200	132	460	210	1600	310	10000	373
65	56	210	136	480	214	1700	313	15000	375
70	59	220	140	500	217	1800	317	20000	377
75	63	230	144	550	225	1900	320	30000	379
80	66	240	148	600	234	2000	322	40000	380
85	70	250	152	650	242	2200	327	50000	381
90	73	260	155	700	248	2400	331	75000	382
95	76	270	159	750	256	2600	335	100000	384

Source: Krejcie and Morgan (1970)

Based on Table 6.2, a sample size for 2,087 is 325 (at 95% confidence interval and 5% margin of error) respondents from 65 vocational colleges. Having identified the sample size, the next step is to choose the appropriate sampling technique that is able to answer all the research questions. Since this study is confirmatory in nature with an adequate population size, the stratified random sampling technique was used.

There are four primary reasons for using stratification (Cochran, 1977):

1. The sub-populations that form the strata are "domains" of study or interest, and thus we need to get separate estimates for each stratum. For example, we may take separate samples for men and women because we are interested in making different inferences for and comparing the sub-populations.

2. The sub-populations or strata are such that different methods or sampling schemes may be suitable for the different strata. For example, if we are estimating the number of words in a textbook, we might take different samples from different sections: the introduction, the main text, the references and the index.

3. The population is geographically diverse, and thus stratification is a convenient way of organizing sampling and data collection.

4. By employing stratification in a careful fashion, we can get improved precision for our estimates of population quantities.

For this study, the 'stratification' was employed due to the geographical reason. By applying the stratified random sampling, the bias issues can be reduced by ensuring that the samples were representatives of the population. Thus, it became valid over the realm it represented, providing the internal validity of the samples. For this research, the bias issue between the samples and the population was minimized. The samples were drawn from the leadership group in vocational colleges, and all colleges participated in the study. The 'random' technique came into the picture when selecting the respondents from each vocational college (drawing the sample from the leadership group).

The procedures for data collection were divided into two phases. The first phase of the data collection was disseminating the questionnaire to the identified vocational colleges for pilot study purposes. The second phase of the data collection involved disseminating the questionnaire to the remaining vocational colleges, which were not involved in the pilot study. Table 6.3 shows the details of the sampling procedures.

The first phase of the data collection process (i.e. the pilot study) was done on 15 vocational colleges (*kolej vokasional rintis*). The remaining 65 vocational colleges participated in the second phase of the data collection with a total sample size of 325. The number of respondents for each vocational college varied due to the random number generated by SPSS.

Table 6.3 Summary of the Sampling Technique and Procedures

Phase	Sampling Technique	Sample Size	No. of Vocational Colleges	No. of Respondents / Vocational College
1 (Pilot Study)	Purposive	225	15	15
2	Stratified Random Sampling	325	65	Based on the random numbers generated by SPSS

INSTRUMENTATION

This subsection elaborates the detailed process of the development and the validation of the questionnaire used in the study including items adaptation and modification, content validation, pilot study and items refinement.

Item Adaptation and Modification

In this study, the instruments were adapted from previous studies. The study used a 5-point Likert scale. Johns (2010) argues that a 5-point Likert scale compromises between offering enough choice (e.g. if only two or three options are used, it tends to measure only direction rather than the strength of opinions) and making things manageable for respondents (less confusion between say, the eighth and ninth point on an eleven-point agree- disagree scale). SL uses a 5-point Likert scale anchored by 1=very untrue of me, 2=untrue of me, 3=neutral, 4=true of me; and 5=very true of me, whilst OB, IST and SA use a 5-point Likert scale anchored by 1= strongly disagree, 2=disagree, 3=neither disagree nor agree, 4=agree and 5=strongly agree.

The survey questionnaire consisted of demographic information of the respondents and four variables under study (i.e. SL, OB, IST and SA). The instrument was divided into five sections. Section A collected the demographic information formed by eight variables (i.e. gender, age, academic qualification, place of work, years of service, current position, grade in current position and years of experience in current position). Section B used adapted instrument to measure SL practices. The statements for measuring SL practices were developed by Hairuddin (2012) based on Davies (2006) and Davies and Davies (2004; 2009). Section B consisted of 48 items comprising of nine dimensions of strategic leadership practices that reflect the respondents themselves. Section C measured the extent of organizational bureaucracy in schools with 51 adapted questionnaires developed by Yucel (1999). Organizational bureaucracy questions measured six bureaucracy dimensions. Section D measured the perceptions of respondents as participants in the in-service training conducted by the Ministry of Education, Malaysia for the past two years. The 27 items measuring in-service training were adapted from the framework of professional development by Guskey (2000a) consisting of five constructs.

Table 6.4 Details of Items to Constructs Investigated

Variables	Constructs Measured	Items
Strategic Leadership Practices	Strategic Orientation	B1-B5
	Strategic Translation	B6-B10
	Strategic Alignment	B11-B15
	Strategic Intervention	B16-B19
	Strategic Competence	B20-B24
	Restlessness	B25-B29
	Absorptive	B30-B34
	Adaptive	B35-B39
	Wisdom	B40-B47
Organizational Bureaucracy	Hierarchy of Authority	C1-C12
	Division of Labor	C13-C19
	Rules and Regulations	C20- C30
	Procedural Specifications	C31-C37
	Formality in Relations	C38-C43
	Promotions based on Technical Competence	C44-C51
In-service Training	Participants' Reactions	D1-D7
	Participants' Learning	D8-D13
	Organization Support and Change	D14-D18
	Participants Use of New Knowledge and Skills	D19-D22
	Students Learning Outcomes	D23-D27
Students' Aspirations	Knowledge	E1-E10
	Thinking Skills	E11(i)-(v)
	Leadership Skills	E12(i)-(viii)
	Bilingual Proficiency	E13-E17
	Ethics and Spirituality	E18-E23
	National Identity	

Sources: Hairuddin (2012), Yucel (1999), Guskey (2000a), Ministry of Education Malaysia (2013).

The last section (i.e. Section E) in the survey was adapted to measure the students' aspiration outcomes from the perspective of the leadership group as teachers precisely looking into the students' aspiration outcomes mentioned by the Malaysian Education Development Plan 2013-2025 (MOE, 2013). It consisted of six constructs with 29-items. Table 6.4 displays the constructs for each variable based on the survey items. Back-translation of the survey questionnaire verified the original translation (Brislin et al., 1973).

Validation Process

In educational research, there are four types of validity that are of much importance. They are face, content, construct and criterion-related validity. This research only takes into consideration face, content and constructs validity. According to Walden (2012), construct validity refers to whether the operational definition of a variable actually reflects the theoretical meaning of a concept. Construct validity comprises two elements namely convergent validity and discriminant validity. This research checks the construct validity using Structural Equation Modelling processes.

Face validity refers to experts' subjective assessments of the presentation and relevance of the measuring instrument. According to Oluwatayo (2012), the criteria for assessment includes:

1. The format of the instrument
2. The clarity or unambiguity of items
3. The appropriateness of difficulty level for the respondents
4. Correct spelling of words
5. Spacing between items
6. Reasonableness of itemsin relation to the perceived purpose of the instrument

The items for the survey instrument were face-validated and content-validated before and during the pilot study. Before the pilot study, the instrument was face- and content- validated by experts at the Kulliyyah of Education, International Islamic University of Malaysia. The selected experts were asked to comment if the items were clear and easy to understand. The researcher also provided a blank space for the experts to comment at the end of each item. The same process was repeated during the pilot study where one respondent was selected from each vocational college to participate in the validation process. All feedbacks were incorporated into the instruments before the final data collection took place.

After the instrument had gone through validation processes, the reliability of the instrument was also tested. Reliability is one of the most desirable technical merits in any educational research. In quantitative research, reliability assures the possibility of replication within a certain limit of experimental error or random error. Thus, if the same methods are used with the same sample, then the results should be the same (Cohen et al., 2008). In a more explicit way, Bowling (2009) views reliability in quantitative research as synonymous with consistency, reproducibility or replicability over time, over instruments and over groups of respondents. There are three types of reliability in educational research: stability, equivalence and internal consistency. This researchused the internal consistency method to measure the reliability of the survey instrument.

DATA COLLECTION PROCEDURE

To collect the data for the study, questionnaires were distributed to all vocational colleges via mail after obtaining permission to enter the research site from the Ministry of Education, Malaysia (specific permission was obtained from two departments, i.e. the Educational Planning and Research Department, and the Technical and Vocational Education Division). Copies of the questionnaire were then distributed via mail directly to every Director of the vocational colleges involved together with a cover letter from the University stating clearly who the respondents are. The list of the respondents was generated by SPSS. Out of 65 vocational colleges, 62 returned the questionnaires. The other three vocational colleges claimed that they had posted the questionnaires but did not reach the researcher. The whole data collection process took three months to complete.

DATA ANALYSIS AND STATISTICAL TECHNIQUE

The study employed various analytical and statistical techniques. Prior to any form of analysis, the collected data underwent a data cleaning process; mainly, outlier detections (inclusive of univariate and multivariate outliers) and normality examination. As mentioned in chapter one, the study seeks to answer 11 research questions. For Research Question 1 (RQ1), descriptive analysis (frequency, mean and standard deviation) was performed. The remainder of the research questions were clarified using Structural Equation Modelling (SEM). SEM was used as the predominant statistical tool due to its capability to estimate series of structural equations, combining both multiple regression analysis and factor analysis features compared to SPSS. Thus, this enabled the researcher to estimate relationships for a complex hypothesized model, taking into consideration the effects of the measurement errors (Hair et al., 2010). The following subsections present data analysis for each research question.

The level of strategic leadership practices, organizational bureaucracy, in-service training effectiveness and students' aspiration outcomes among vocational educational leaders

The level of strategic leadership practices, organizational bureaucracy, in-service training effectiveness and students' aspiration outcomes among vocational educational leaders are measured by RQ1. The result of RQ1 highlights the level of strategic leadership practices, the level of organizational bureaucracy, in-service training effectiveness and the level of students' aspiration outcomes at present from the perspective of the vocational educational leaders. The study uses frequency, means and standard deviation to answer this question.

The validity and reliability of the strategic leadership practices measurement model

RQ2 investigates the psychometric properties, reliability, and validity of a nine-construct model of strategic leadership practices. Hypothesis 1 (the strategic leadership practices measurement model is valid and reliable) demonstrates that the nine-construct measurement model holds psychometric evidence, is valid and reliable constituting strategic leadership practices. The outcome of RQ2 leads to adequate instruments of strategic leadership practices.

The validity and reliability of the organizational bureaucracy measurement model

RQ3 investigates the psychometric properties, reliability and validity of a six-construct model of organizational bureaucracy. Hypothesis 2 (the level of organizational bureaucracy measurement model is valid and reliable) demonstrates that the six-construct measurement model holds psychometric evidence, is valid and reliable constituting organizational bureaucracy. The outcome of RQ3 leads to the adequate instruments of organizational bureaucracy.

The validity and reliability of the in-service training effectiveness measurement model

RQ4 investigates the psychometric properties, reliability, and validity of a five-construct model of in-service training effectiveness. Hypothesis 3 (The in-service training effectiveness measurement model is valid and reliable) demonstrates that the five-construct measurement model holds psychometric evidence, is valid and reliable constituting in-service training effectiveness. The outcome of RQ4 leads to the adequate instruments of in-service training effectiveness.

The validity and reliability of the students' aspiration outcomes measurement model

RQ5 investigates the psychometric properties, reliability, and validity of a six-construct model of students' aspiration outcomes. Hypothesis 4 (the students' aspiration outcomes measurement model is valid and reliable) demonstrates that the six-construct measurement model holds psychometric evidence, valid and reliable constituting students' aspiration outcomes. The outcome of RQ5 leads to the adequate instruments of students' aspiration outcomes. Each of the four measurement models above should display at least four of the recommended GOF indices shown in Table 6.5.

Reliability, validity and psychometric properties of the students' aspiration outcomes measurement model were evaluated by using PCA factor loadings, CFA, AVE, and CRI. The construct validity of the students' aspiration outcomes measurement model was tested using PCA and CFA whilst the psychometric properties, validity and reliability were evaluated through the calculation of AVE and CRI. The constructs are valid and reliable if AVE and CRI are fulfilled and the measurement model fits the observed data.

Table 6.5 Summary of the GOF Indices

Index	Description	Conventional Value	Recent Recommendation
NFI	Sample-based.	≥.90	.95
NNFI	Sample-based, value can fall outside of range 0 -1.0.	≥.90	.95
TLI	Not associated with sample size. Values can exceed 1.0, but truncated to 1.0 if it does.	≥.90	.95
PCFI	Population-based. Sensitive to sample size.	≥.90	.95
RNI	Population-based. Value can be negative.	≥.90	.95
GFI	Sample-based. Value can fall outside range of 0 -1.0.	≥.90	.95
Chi-square (χ^2)	Based on a test that provides a statistical test that produces difference.	-	-
δf	The amount of mathematical information available to estimate model parameters.	-	-
RMSEA	Corrects χ^2 goodness-of-fit for models with large sample.	≤.08	.06
SRMR	Compares fit across two models. The average value is 0.	The lower the value, the better.	-
RMSR	Compare two models. Normally used when the results are standardized.	-	-
PGFI	The value ranges between 0 and 1.	.90	-
PNFI	Adjust the NFI by multiplying it by the parsimony ratio. Model-based.	.90	-

Source: Hair et al. (2010); Kline (2011); Hu and Bentler (1999).

Relationship between strategic leadership practices and students' aspiration outcomes

RQ6 attempts to establish the direct causal effect of strategic leadership practices on students' aspiration outcomes. Hypothesis 5 (there is a direct and significant relationship between strategic leadership practices and students' aspiration outcomes) attempts to prove that strategic leadership practices have a direct causal effect on students' aspiration outcomes.

Relationship between organizational bureaucracy and students' aspiration outcomes

RQ7 attempts to establish the direct causal effect of organizational bureaucracy on student's aspiration outcomes. Therefore, Hypothesis 6 (There is a direct and significant relationship between organizational bureaucracy and student's aspiration outcomes)

Attempts to prove that organizational bureaucracy has a direct causal effect on students' aspiration outcomes.

Relationship between in-service training effectiveness and students' aspiration outcomes

RQ8 attempts to establish the direct causal effect of in-service training effectiveness on student's aspiration outcomes. Therefore, Hypothesis 7 (There is a direct and significant relationship between in-service training effectiveness and students' aspiration outcomes) attempts to prove that in-service training effectiveness has a direct causal effect on students' aspiration outcomes.

As with RQ6 and RQ7, the relationship in RQ8 is between two latent variables. Thus, within SEM functionality, the direct causal effect was used to investigate the strength of the two latent variables. The direct causal effect value needs to be between 0 and 1 at 0.05 significant level.

The mediation effect of organizational bureaucracy on strategic leadership practices and students' aspiration outcomes.

RQ9 attempts to establish the indirect effect of strategic leadership practices on students' aspiration outcomes. Therefore, Hypothesis 8 (organizational bureaucracy mediates the relationship between strategic leadership practices and student's aspiration outcomes) attempts to demonstrate how strategic leadership practices influence students' aspiration outcomes through organizational bureaucracy. To answer RQ9, the significant indirect effect of strategic leadership practices on students' aspiration outcomes were investigated by evaluating the strength of relationship among strategic leadership practices, organizational bureaucracy, and students' aspiration outcomes.

As with RQ9, the investigation involved confirming the relationship between three latent variables. Thus, within SEM functionality, the indirect causal effect was used to investigate the strength of the relationship. The indirect causal effect value needs to be between 0 and 1 at 0.05 significant level.

The mediation effect of in-service training effectiveness on strategic leadership practices and students' aspiration outcomes

RQ10 attempts to establish the indirect effect of strategic leadership practices on students' aspiration outcomes. Therefore, Hypothesis 9 (In-service training effectiveness mediates the relationship between strategic leadership practices and students' aspiration outcomes) attempts to demonstrate how strategic leadership practices influence students' aspiration outcomes through in-service training effectiveness. To answer RQ10, the significant indirect effect of strategic leadership practices on students' aspiration outcomes was investigated through evaluating the strength of relationship among strategic leadership practices, in-service training effectiveness, and students' aspiration outcomes. As with RQ9, the investigation involves confirming the relationship between three latent variables. Thus, within SEM functionality, as with RQ9, the indirect causal effect was used to investigate the strength of the relationship in which the indirect causal effect value needs to be between 0 and 1 at 0.05 significant level.

The validity and reliability of the revised hypothesized structural equation model of TVESAI

RQ11 assesses the relationship among the four validated measurement models above. Therefore, Hypothesis 10 (the revised hypothesized structural equation model of TVESAI is valid and reliable) attempts to test and validate the directional causal effect of the hypothesized model of this research. Thus, within SEM functionality, the hypothesized model was revised to obtain the best fitting model. The analysis was conducted by obtaining the goodness-of-fit (GOF) of the competing models. SEM fit indices, and changes in Chi-square (c^2) values were used to determine the model fit. The summary of the statistical technique is tabulated in Table 6.6.

Table 6.6 Summary of the Statistical Techniques

Research Question	Statistical Technique
• *RQ1*	• Mean, frequency, standard deviation
• *RQ2*	• CFA
• *RQ3*	• CFA
• *RQ4*	• CFA
• *RQ5*	• CFA
• *RQ6*	• Structural Equation Model
• *RQ7*	• Structural Equation Model
• *RQ8*	• Structural Equation Model
• *RQ9*	• Structural Equation Model
• *RQ10*	• Structural Equation Model
• *RQ11*	• Full-fledged Model

CHAPTER SEVEN

ANALYSIS OF THE SAMPLED DATA AND RESULTS

INTRODUCTION

After the data had been screened and cleaned, the analysis process continued with the descriptive analysis of the sampled data. This chapter was divided into two parts: demographic profile of the respondents and descriptive analysis of the level of strategic leadership practices, the level of organizational bureaucracy, in-service training effectiveness and the level of students' aspiration outcomes among vocational educational leaders.

DEMOGRAPHIC PROFILES OF THE RESPONDENTS

Of the 343 respondents in this study, 47.8% are males, and 52.2% are females. The age of the respondents ranged from 20 to 59 years old, 4.7% are between 20 and 29 years old, 28.9% are between 30 and 39 years old, 41.0% were between 40 and 49 years old and the remaining 25.4% are between 50 and 59 years old. Regarding the respondents' academic qualification, one respondent held a doctoral degree (.3%), while 16.3% respondents had Master's degrees. The majority of the respondents (80.4%) are first-degree holders. The maining1.2% and 1.8% respondents are diploma holders and had other academic qualifications respectively.

As for the respondents' years of service, 13.7% had served the government for 1-9 years, 36.2% between 10-19 years, 41.6% between 20-29 years and 8.5% had served the government for more than 30 years. Pertaining to the respondents' current leadership position, 1.2% of the respondents are Directors of the vocational colleges, 8.5% are Deputy Directors, 21% held Head of Department's position, the majority of the respondents are Head of Units, and 10.8% held other leadership positions. Finally, in terms of the years of service in the current leadership position, 4.1% had been in the leadership position for less than a year, 81.3% had been in the leadership position between 1-9 years, 7.3% had served between 10-19 years in leadership positions, 3.8% between 20-29 years and 3.5% of the respondents had been in the leadership position for more than 30 years. The details of the respondents according to gender, age, academic qualification, years of service, current position and years in the current leadership position are tabulated in Table 7.1.

Table 7.1 Demographic Profiles of the Respondents

Variables	n	%
Gender		
Male	164	47.8
Female	179	52.2
Age		
20-29 years old	16	4.7
30-39 years old	99	28.9
40-49 years old	141	41.0
50-59 years old	87	25.4
Academic Qualifications		
PhD	1	.3
Master's degrees	56	16.3
Bachelor degrees	276	80.4
Diplomas	4	1.2
Others	6	1.8
Years of Service		
1-9 years	47	13.7
10-19 years	124	36.2
20-29 years	143	41.6
30-39 years	29	8.5
Current Leadership Position		
Director	4	1.2
Deputy Director	29	8.5
Head of Department	72	21.0
Head of Unit	201	58.5
Others	37	10.8
Years in Current Leadership Position		
< 1 year	14	4.1
1-9 years	279	81.3
10-19 years	25	7.3
20-29 years	13	3.8
> 30 years	12	3.5

Note: N = 343

DESCRIPTIVE ANALYSIS OF THE LEVEL OF STRATEGIC LEADERSHIP PRACTICES, LEVEL OF ORGANIZATIONAL BUREAUCRACY, IN-SERVICE TRAINING EFFECTIVENESS AND LEVEL OF STUDENTS' ASPIRATION OUTCOMES

This section describes the level of SL practices, the level of OB, IST effectiveness and the level of SA among vocational leaders in terms of the mean and standard deviation of each construct. It addresses RQ1 (What is the level of strategic leadership practices (SL), the level of organizational bureaucracy (OB), in-service training effectiveness (IST) and level of students' aspiration outcomes (SA) among vocational educational leaders?) Table 7.2 summarizes the mean, standard deviation, skewness, kurtosis and the internal reliability of each construct.

Table 7.2 Mean, Standard Deviation, Skewness, Kurtosis and Internal Reliability of Each Construct

Variables	Constructs Measured	No of items	Mean	SD	Kurtosis	Skewness	Internal Reliability
Strategic Leadership Practices	Strategic Orientation	5	4.184	.4578	-.006	-.247	.822
	Strategic Translation	5	4.002	.4653	.002	.125	.798
	Strategic Alignment	5	4.045	.4719	.146	-.042	.839
	Strategic Intervention	4	3.930	.4716	-.027	.393	.763
	Strategic Competence	5	4.089	.4360	.162	.031	.797
	Restlessness	5	4.221	.4403	.132	-.316	.818
	Absorptive	5	4.129	.4366	.132	-.033	.763
	Adaptive	5	4.176	.4312	.111	-.204	.812
	Wisdom	8	4.207	.4142	-.049	-.060	.858
Organizational Bureaucracy	Hierarchy of Authority	12	3.636	.5148	-.205	-.090	.828
	Division of Labor	4	2.358	.7950	.492	-.304	.678
	Rules and Regulations	9	4.147	.3811	.159	.158	.831
	Procedural Specifications	7	3.570	.5439	-.003	.259	.759
	Impersonality	4	3.865	.5587	-.523	.954	.659
	Technical Competence	5	3.938	.4562	-.003	.382	.614
In-service Training	Participants' Reactions	7	4.075	.3818	.416	.744	.818
	Participants' Learning	5	4.075	.4217	.375	.285	.823
	Organization Support and Change	6	3.826	.4189	-.287	.932	.797
	Participants Use of New Knowledge and Skills	4	4.047	.4112	.289	.940	.813
	Student's Learning Outcomes	4	3.856	.4472	.045	.544	.820
Students' Aspirations	Knowledge	8	3.864	.5130	.011	-.084	.820
	Thinking Skills	5	3.412	.6745	-.314	-.297	.866
	Leadership Skills	8	3.683	.5325	-.006	-.062	.803
	Bilingual Proficiency	10	3.578	.4804	-.162	.158	.803
	Ethics and Spirituality	4	4.209	.4991	-.126	-.529	.676
	National Identity	6	3.852	.5055	.089	-.083	.815

Table 7.2 shows that for the level of strategic leadership practices (organizational capabilities), the highest score is for strategic orientation (M = 4.184, SD = .4578), followed by strategic competencies (M = 4.089, SD = .4360), strategic alignment (M = 4.045, SD = .4719), strategic translation (M = 4.002, SD = .4653) while the lowest score is for strategic intervention (M = 3.930, SD = .4716). For the level of strategic leadership practices (individual characteristics), the highest score is restlessness (M = 4.221, SD = .4403), followed by wisdom (M = 4.207, SD = .4142), adaptive capacity (M = 4.176, .4312), and absorptive capacity (M = 4.129, SD = .4366).

For the level of organizational bureaucracy, the highest score is for rules and regulations (M = 4.147, SD = .3811), while the lowest score is for division of labour (M = 2.358, SD = .7950). In between the two constructs are technical competencies (M = 3.938, SD = .4562), impersonality (M = 3.865, SD = .5587), hierarchy of authority (M = 3.636, SD = .5148) and procedural specification (M = 3.570, SD = .5439).

As for the in-service training effectiveness, the highest score is participants' learning (M = 4.075, SD = .3818) and participants' reaction (M = 4.075, SD = .4217). The second highest score is participants' use of new knowledge and skills (M = 4.047, SD = .4112), followed by students' learning outcomes (M = 3.856, SD = .4472) and lastly, organization support and change (M = 3.826, SD = .4189).

Lastly, for the level of students' aspirations from the vocational leaders' perspective, the highest score is for ethics and spirituality (M = 4.209, SD = .4991), followed by knowledge (M = 3.864, SD = .5130), national identity (M = 3.852, SD = .5055), leadership skills (M = 3.683, SD = .5325), bilingual proficiency (M = 3.578, SD = .4804) and thinking skills (M = 3.412, SD = .6745).

In general, the level of strategic leadership practices is high with the mean values ranging from 4.221 (restlessness) to 3.930 (strategic intervention). Similarly, the level of in-service training effectiveness is also on the high side with the mean values ranging from 4.075 (participant's learning and participant's reaction) to 3.826 (organization support and change). However, the level of organizational bureaucracy is moderate compared to the level of strategic leadership and in-service training effectiveness with the mean values ranging from 4.147 (rules and regulations) to 3.570 (procedural specification). In addition, the level of students' aspirations from the vocational leaders' perspective is also moderate with the mean values ranging from 4.209 (ethics and spirituality) to 3.412 (thinking skills). Based on the above discussion, RQ1 is fully addressed.

TEST OF STATISTICAL ASSUMPTIONS

As with all statistical methodologies, SEM requires that certain underlying assumptions be satisfied to ensure accurate inferences (Kaplan, 2009). These include multivariate normality, completely random missing data, sufficiently large sample size, and correct model specification. As the issues of missing data and sample size have been discussed in the earlier part of the discussion, this subsection concentrates on testing the normality of the sampled data. Model specification is also elaborated in the subsequent subsection.

There are two ways of testing normality assumption, i.e. Levene's test or skewness and kurtosis. This research used the second method of testing the normality of the sampled data. Skewness represents the symmetry of the data distribution. When a variable's mean is not at the centre of the distribution, it is skewed. Kurtosis however, is the peakedness of distribution (Tabachnick & Fidell, 2007; Schumacker & Lomax, 1996). Distribution is either too peaked (with short and thick tails) or too flat (with long and thick tails). The rule of thumb of using skewness and kurtosis analysis is that for a variable dataset to reasonably be close to normal, the skewness and kurtosis values need to be between -1.0 and +1.0 (Meyers et al., 2006; Tabachnick & Fidell, 2007).

Based on Table 7.2, the analyses show that the skewness and kurtosis of the variables under study fell within the recommended cut-off values. Therefore, the data set did not violate the normality assumptions.

RESULTS OF THE CONFIRMATORY FACTOR ANALYSIS (CFA) FOR EACH VARIABLE

This subsection addresses Research Questions 2-5 by testing the first four hypotheses of this study. In order to test the hypotheses, Confirmatory Factor Analysis (CFA) was used. To confirm whether each hypothesis is supported, the multi-dimensional constructs of each variable should at least possess any three goodness-of-fit indices (Hair, 2010) in order to provide adequate evidence of model fit. Subsequently, each construct should indicate convergent validity (average variance extract (AVE) $\geq$ .5 and composite reliability (CR) $\geq$ .7) of the hypothesized model. After both conditions are fulfilled, then, it can be concluded that the hypothesized model is valid and reliable.

CFA for Multi-Dimensional Constructs of Strategic Leadership Practices (SI)

The first variable to be analysed was the strategic leadership practices constructs by Davies (2006) and Davies and Davies (2004; 2009). Davies (2006) and Davies and Davies (2004; 2009)which suggest that strategic leadership practices consist of two components; organizational capabilities (ORG) and individual characteristics (INDV). Each component has five and four constructs respectively. Therefore, from SEM's interpretation, the component is analysed separately by CFA and later, the two components were combined to confirm whether a second order model exists. Otherwise, the further analysis considers strategic leadership practices as a one-dimensional construct. With that, the first CFA is for ORG followed by CFA for INDV.

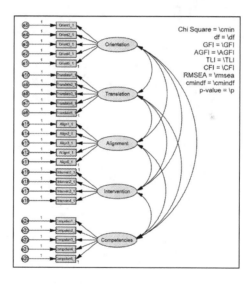

Figure 7.1 Hypothesized Multi-dimensional Constructs of Organizational Capabilities (ORG)

Note. Orientation = Strategic Orientation, *Translation* = Strategic Translation, *Alignment* = Strategic Alignment, *Intervention* = Strategic Intervention and *Competencies* = Strategic Competencies.

The first part of the first variable evaluated using CFA belongs to ORG. ORG consists of five underlying constructs which are the Strategic Orientation (*Orientation*), Strategic Translation (*Translation*), Strategic Alignment (*Alignment*), Strategic Intervention (*Intervention*), and Strategic Competencies (*Competencies*). All constructs were measured by five items except *Intervention*, which has four items. All 24 items were hypothesized to load on sub-scales of the ORG constructs. Figure 7.1 depicts the hypothesized ORG multi-dimensional constructs.

The interrelationships among all 24 items were statistically significant. The data do not violate the assumption of normality with skewness between ±2 (Tabachnick & Fidell, 2007) and kurtosis between ±7 (Byrne, 2010). The five constructs show poor model fit, χ^2 (242) = 716.062, p = .000 which is statistically significant, indicating an inadequate fit between the covariance matrix of the observed data and the implied covariance matrix of the model.

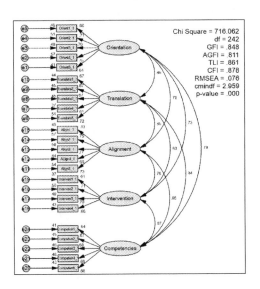

Figure 7.2 Generated Multi-dimensional Constructs of Organizational Capabilities (ORG)

Note. Orientation = Strategic Orientation, *Translation* = Strategic Translation, *Alignment* = Strategic Alignment, *Intervention* = Strategic Intervention and *Competencies* = Strategic Competencies.

Other fit indices are also found to hold inadequate values. The GFI = .848, CFI = .878 and TLI = .861 fell below the threshold value of ≥. 90. However, the normed $\chi^2/\partial f$ = 2.959 and the RMSEA value = .076 fall between the acceptable range of ≤ 3 and ≤ .08 respectively. Furthermore, the parameter estimate of loadings range from .608 to .733. Thus, the model does not fit the sample data. Figure 7.2depicts the generated hypothesized ORG multi-dimensional constructs.

All loadings are above .5 but the initial hypothesized model is invalid based on the fit indices. Therefore, the next step was to drop items with standardized residuals larger than 4 and the generated multi-dimensional constructs of ORG was re-specified. Out of five items of *Orientation*, three items were dropped. Similarly, one item was dropped for *Alignment,* and one item was dropped for *Intervention*. All items for *Translation* and *Competencies* were dropped. Thus the two constructs were eliminated from the multi-dimensional constructs of ORG. In total, 15 items out of 24 were dropped to achieve model fit.

The overall re-specified model shows an improved goodness-of-fit indices, which is consistent with the data. The goodness-of-fit of the re-specified model is substantial. The normed $\chi^2/\partial f = 2.876$ and the RMSEA value = .074 fall between the acceptable range of ≤ 3 and $\leq .08$ respectively, which reflect a good fit of the revised model. Other fit indices is also found to hold adequate values. The GFI = .962, CFI = .967 and TLI = .946 was above the threshold value of $\geq .90$. Table 7.3 compares the result of the fit indices of the generated model, the re-specified model against the recommended threshold values.

Table 7.3. Summary of the Fit Indices of the Multi-
dimensional Constructs of ORG

Fit Indices	Accepted fit	ORG Generated Model	ORG Re-specified Model
• Chi-square	Insignificant	2557.176	268.596
• *p* value*	$.001 \leq p \leq .05$	.000	.000
• CMIN/DF	≤ 3	2.959	2.876
• CFI	$\geq .90$	.878	.967
• TLI	$\geq .90$	.861	.946
• GFI	$\geq .90$	.848	.962
• RMSEA	$\leq .08$	.076	.074

*Source: Kline (2011); Schumacker and Lomax (1996); Hair et al. (2010); Hu and Bentler (1995); Byrne (2010) *Statistically significant at .05.*

Based on Table 7.3, the re-specified model of the multi-dimensional constructs of ORG fell within the range of the accepted fit indices values. Thus, indicating an adequate fit between the covariance matrix of the observed data and the implied covariance matrix of the model.

In addition, the parameter estimates were also examined and were found to be statistically significant. The loadings range from .678 (*Interven1_1*) to .777 (*Interven2_1*). They were free from any offending estimates and showed a logical direction. The values of the squared multiple correlations (SMC) range from .460 (*Interven1_1*) to .604 (*Interven2_1*). The SMC indicates how well the items serve as the manifests of the constructs and provide evidence of the reliability of the items investigated (Blunch, 2008). It is worth noting that all the values of the SMC for the revised multi-dimensional are above .25, thus, portraying substantial evidence of the variance in the nine observed items of the revised multi-dimensional constructs of ORG. Figure 7.3 depicts the re-specified ORG multi-dimensional constructs.

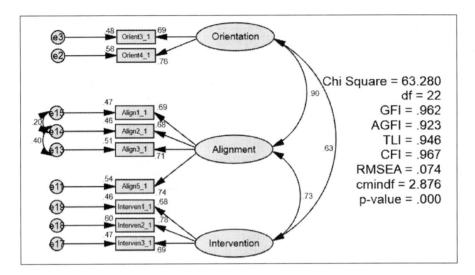

Figure 7.3: Re-specified Multi-dimensional Constructs of Organizational Capabilities (ORG)

Note. Orientation = Strategic Orientation, *Alignment* = Strategic Alignment and *Intervention* = Strategic Intervention.

The re-specified multi-dimensional constructs of ORG fit the sample data. Further analysis is required to test the convergent validity of the hypothesized model. Table 7.4 summarizes the internal reliability, the factor loadings, the average variance extract (AVE) and the composite reliability (CR) for the revised hypothesized model of ORG.

Table 7.4 Summary of the Convergent Validity of the Re-specified Multi-dimensional Constructs of ORG

Constructs	Items	Internal Reliability (Cronbach Alpha)	Factor Loading	AVE	CR
Orientation	Orient3_1	.687	.69	.527	.690
	Orient4_1		.76		
Alignment	Align1_1		.71		
	Align2_1	.830	.72	.518	.812
	Align3_1		.72		
	Align5_1		.73		
Intervention	Interven1_1		.68		
	Interven2_1	.754	.78	.516	.761
	Interven3_1		.69		

Note. Orientation = Strategic Orientation, *Alignment* = Strategic Alignment and *Intervention* = Strategic Intervention.

From the above table, all constructs have AVE values ≥ .5 and CR values ≥ .7, respectively. Thus, the re-specified multi-dimensional constructs of ORG have the evidence of convergent validity. Based on the fit indices and the convergent validity of the re-specified ORG multi-dimensional constructs, the analysis reveals that the constructs of ORG were valid and reliable.

The second part of the first variable evaluated using CFA belongs to individual characteristics (INDV). INDV consists of four underlying constructs, which are the Restlessness (Restlessness), Absorptive Capacity (*Absorptive*), Adaptive Capacity (*Adaptive*) and Wisdom (*Wisdom*). All constructs are measured by five items except *Wisdom*, which has eight items. All 23 items were hypothesized to load on sub-scales of the INDV constructs. Figure 7.4 depicts the hypothesized INDV multi-dimensional constructs.

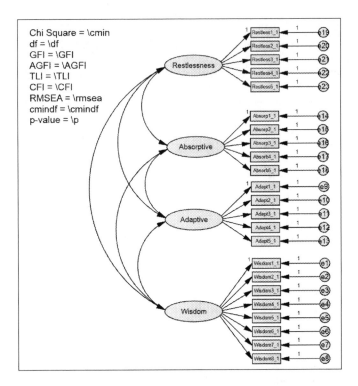

Figure 7.4 Hypothesized Multi-dimensional Constructs of Individual Characteristics (INDV)

Note. Restlessness = Restlessness, *Absorptive* = Absorptive Capacity, *Adaptive* = Adaptive Capacity and *Wisdom* = Wisdom.

The inter relationships among all 23 items are statistically significant. The data does not violate the assumption of normality with skewness between ±2 (Tabachnick & Fidell, 2007) and kurtosis between ±7 (Byrne, 2010). The four constructs show poor model fit, χ^2 (224) = 917.430, p = .000 which is statistically significant, indicating an inadequate fit between the covariance matrix of the observed data and the implied covariance matrix of the model.

Other fit indices are also found to hold inadequate values. The GFI = .763, CFI = .829 and TLI = .807 fall below the threshold value of ≥. 90. In addition, the normed $\chi^2/\partial f$ = 4.096 and the RMSEA value = .095 are out of the acceptable range of ≤ 3 and ≤ .08, respectively. The parameter estimate of loadings range from .382 to .774. Loadings should not be below .5 (Byrne, 2010). Thus, the model does not fit the sample data. Figure 7.5 depicts the generated INDV multi-dimensional constructs.

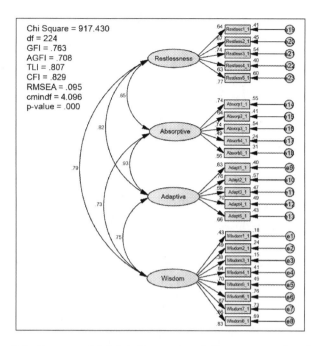

Figure 7.5: Generated Multi-dimensional Constructs of Individual Characteristics (INDV)

Note. Restlessness = Restlessness, *Absorptive* = Absorptive Capacity, *Adaptive* = Adaptive Capacity and *Wisdom* = Wisdom.

The decision was made to drop loadings that were below .5 for better model fit. Therefore, the generated multi-dimensional constructs of INDV were re-specified. Out of five items of *Restlessness*, two items were dropped. Similarly, two items were dropped for *Absorptive*, two items were dropped for *Adaptive* and five items were dropped for *Wisdom*. In total, 11 items out of 23 were dropped to achieve model fit.

The overall re-estimated model shows an improved goodness-of-fit indices, which are consistent with the data. The goodness-of-fit indices of the re-specified model are substantial. The normed $\chi^2/\partial f$ = 2.515 and the RMSEA value = .067 fall between the acceptable range of $\leq$ 3 and $\leq$ .08 respectively, which reflected a good fit in the revised model. Other fit indices are also found to hold adequate values. The GFI = .941, CFI = .967 and TLI = .955 are above the threshold value of $\geq$. 90. Table 7.5 compares the result of the fit indices of the generated model, the re-specified model against the recommended threshold values.

Table 7.5 Summary of the Fit Indices of the Multi-dimensional Constructs of INDV

Fit Indices	Accepted fit	INDV Initial Model	INDV Revised Model
• Chi-square	Insignificant	917.430	120.703
• p value*	$.001 \leq p \leq .05$	.000	.000
• CMIN/DF	≤ 3	4.096	2.515
• CFI	$\geq .90$	.829	.967
• TLI	$\geq .90$	.807	.955
• GFI	$\geq .90$	.763	.941
• RMSEA	$\leq .08$	.095	.067

Source: Kline (2011); Schumacker and Lomax (1996); Hair et al. (2010); Hu and Bentler (1995); Byrne (2010)
* Statistically significant at .05

Based on Table 7.5, the re-specified model of the multi-dimensional constructs of INDV fell within the range of the accepted fit indices values. Thus, indicating an adequate fit between the covariance matrix of the observed data and the implied covariance matrix of the model.

In addition, the parameter estimates were also examined and were found to be statistically significant. The loadings ranged from .631 (*Absorp2_1*) to .914 (*Wisdom7_1*). They are free from any offending estimates and showed logical directions. The values of the squared multiple correlations (SMC) range from .399 (*Absorp2_1*) to .835 (*Wisdom7_1*). It is worth noting that all values of the SMC for the revised multi-dimensional are above .25, thus, giving substantial evidence of the variance in the 12 items of the revised multi-dimensional constructs of INDV. Figure 7.6 depicts the re-specified INDV multi-dimensional constructs.

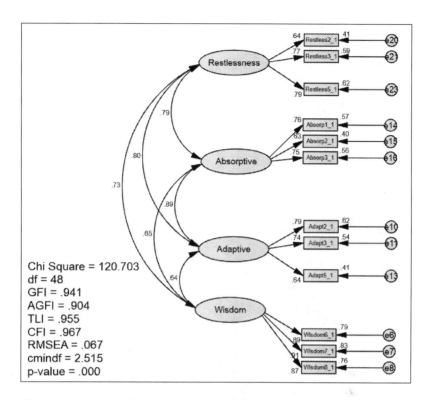

Figure 7.6 Re-specified Multi-dimensional Constructs of Individual Characteristics (INDV)

Note. Restlessness = Restlessness, *Absorptive* = Absorptive Capacity, *Adaptive* = Adaptive Capacity and *Wisdom* = Wisdom.

Based on Figure 7.6, the re-specified multi-dimensional constructs of INDV fit the sample data. Further analysis is required to test the convergent validity of the hypothesized model. Table 7.6 summarizes the internal reliability, the factor loadings, the average variance extract (AVE) and the composite reliability (CR) for the re-specified hypothesized model of INDV.

From the above table, all constructs had AVE values ≥ .5 and CR values ≥ .7, respectively. Thus, the re-specified multi-dimensional constructs of INDV show the evidence of convergent validity. Based on the fit indices and the convergent validity of the re-specified hypothesized INDV multi-dimensional constructs, the analysis reveals that the constructs of INDV were valid and reliable.

Table 7.6 Summary of the Convergent Validity of the Re-specified Multi-dimensional Constructs of IND

Constructs	Items	Internal Reliability (Cronbach Alpha)	Factor Loading	AVE	CR
Restlessness	Restless2_1		.64		
	Restless3_1	.776	.77	.542	.779
	Restless5_1		.79		
Absorptive	Absorp1_1		.76		
	Absorp2_1	.761	.63	.512	.758
	Absorp3_1		.75		
Adaptive	Adapt2_1		.79		
	Adapt3_1	.764	.74	.527	.768
	Adapt5_1		.64		
Wisdom	Wisdom6_1		.89		
	Wisdom7_1	.762	.91	.792	.920
	Wisdom8_1		.87		

Note. Restlessness = Restlessness, *Absorptive* = Absorptive Capacity, *Adaptive* = Adaptive Capacity and *Wisdom* = Wisdom.

The CFA results of the re-specified ORG and INDV multi-dimensional constructs were further analysed for a second-order model of strategic leadership practices. The re-specified ORG multi-dimensional constructs consist of three constructs with nine items while INDV multi-dimensional constructs consist of four constructs with 12 items. For the second-order model, the item-parceling technique was used. Item parcelling involves summing up items as indicators of the latent constructs. Thus, the second-order model of strategic leadership practices is hypothesized as a two-dimensional construct consisting of ORG and INDV with three and four summated scores latent factor, respectively. Figure 7.7 depicts the generated second-order model for strategic leadership practices.

Based on Figure 7.7, the second-order generated model shows excellent goodness-of-fit indices, which are consistent with the data. The normed $\chi^2/\partial f$ = 2.948 and the RMSEA value = .075 fall between the acceptable range of ≤ 3 and ≤ .08 respectively, which reflects a good fit in the revised model. Other fit indices are also found to hold adequate values. The GFI = .968, CFI = .979 and TLI = .966 are above the threshold value of ≥. 90. However, the parameter estimate of SL → ORG indicates a value of 2.53 which gave a sign of offending estimate (the parameter estimate should not be more than 1). In addition, the error variance of e8 indicates negative value of -.844 (error variance should be a positive value). Thus, it can be concluded that, the second-order model of strategic leadership practices did not exist.

From now on, strategic leadership practices were considered as a one-dimensional model with seven summated latent constructs. To confirm that the strategic leadership practices were a uni-dimensional model, CFA was run to validate the goodness-of-fit indices. Figure 7.8depicts the re-specified one-dimensional model of strategic leadership practices.

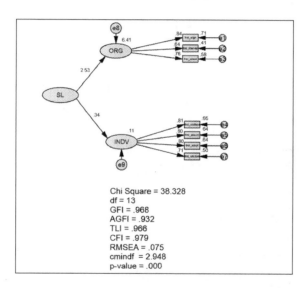

Chi Square = 38.328
df = 13
GFI = .968
AGFI = .932
TLI = .966
CFI = .979
RMSEA = .075
cmindf = 2.948
p-value = .000

Figure 7.7 Generated Second-Order Model of Strategic Leadership Practices (SL)

Note. SL = Strategic Leadership Practices, ORG = Organizational Capabilities,INDV = Individual Characteristics, *first_align* = Strategic Alignment, *first_interven* = Strategic Intervention, *first_orient* = Strategic Orientation, *first_restless* = Restlessness, *first_absorp* = Absorptive Capacity, *first adapt* = Adaptive Capacity and *first_Wisdom* = Wisdom.

Based on Figure 7.8, the re-specified one-dimensional model of SL consists of seven summated latent constructs, i.e. strategic alignment, strategic intervention, strategic orientation, restlessness, absorptive capacity, adaptive capacity and wisdom. To improve the model fit, two inter-correlations among four errors were freed based on the suggestions of Modification Indices (MIs). More specifically, the following connections were established error 1 (*first_align*) with error 3 (*first_orient*) and error 5 (*first_absorp*) with error 6 (*first_adapt*). Methodologically, in AMOS, the error correlations show a sign of communalities between the observed variables.

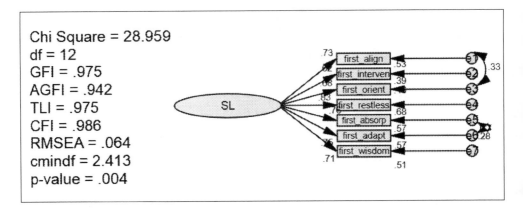

Figure 7.8 Re-specified One-Dimensional Model of Strategic Leadership Practices (SL)

Note. SL = Strategic Leadership Practices, *first_align* = Strategic Alignment, *first_interven* = Strategic Intervention, *first_orient* = Strategic Orientation, *first_restless* = Restlessness, *first_absorp* = Absorptive Capacity, *first adapt* = Adaptive Capacity and *first_Wisdom*= Wisdom.

The overall results show that the goodness-of-fit indices of the re-specified one-dimensional model of SL are consistent with the sampled data. The χ^2 is statistically significant (12) = 28.959, *p* = .004, implying an adequate fit between the covariance matrix of the observed data and the implied covariance matrix of the model. Although the χ^2 is statistically significant, the re-specified model fits the observed data since the value of the normed $\chi^2/\partial f$ = 2.413, and the RMSEA value = .064 fell between the acceptable range of ≤ 3 and ≤ .08 respectively, which reflects good fit in the revised model. Other fit indices are also found to hold adequate values. The GFI = .975, CFI = .986 and TLI = .975 are above the threshold value of ≥. 90.

The parameter estimate of loadings ranged from .62 (*first_interven*) to .83 (*first_restless*). They are free from any offending estimates and showed logical directions. The values of the squared multiple correlations (SMC) ranged from .387 (*first_interven*) to .683 (*first_restless*). It is worth noting that all the values of the SMC for the re-specified multi-dimensional are above .25. Thus, it gave substantial evidence of the variance for the seven items of the one-dimensional model of SL. Based on the fit indices of the re-specified one-dimensional model of SL, the analysis reveals that Hypothesis 1 is supported with the finding that the measurement model of SL is valid and reliable. Thus, Research Question 2 is fully addressed.

CFA for Multi-Dimensional Constructs of Organizational Bureaucracy (OB)

The second construct evaluated using CFA belongs to OB. OB consists of six underlying factors which are the Hierarchy of Authority (HA), Rules and Regulation (RR), Procedural Specification (PS), Technical Competencies (TC), Impersonality (IM) and Division of Labor (DL). HA was measured by 12 indicator variables. The second factor, RR was measured by ten indicator variables. The third factor, PS was measured by seven indicator variables. The fourth factor, TC was measured by six indicator variables and the fifth and sixth factors, IM and DL were measured with five and four indicator variables, respectively. All 44 items were hypothesized to load on sub-scales of the OB latent constructs. Figure 7.9 depicts the hypothesized OB multi-dimensional constructs.

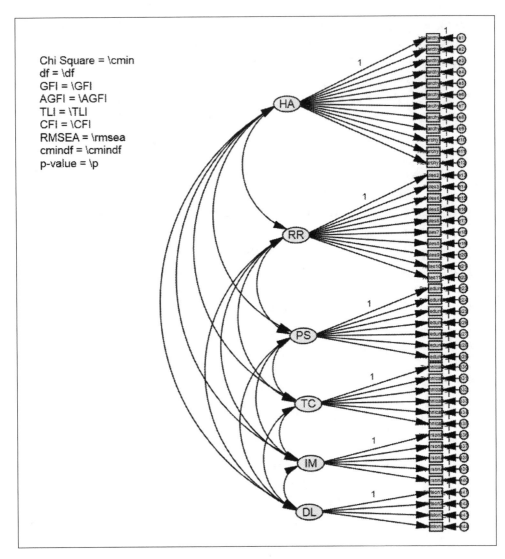

Figure 7.9 Hypothesized Multi-dimensional Constructs of Organizational Bureaucracy (OB)

Note. HA = Hierarchy of Authority, RR = Rules and Regulation, PS = Procedural Specification, TC = Technical Competencies, IM = Impersonality and DL = Division of Labor.

The interrelationships among all 44 indicators are statistically significant except for *Rules10_1*. The data does not violate the assumption of normality with skewness between ±2 (Tabachnick & Fidell, 2007) and kurtosis between ±7 (Byrne, 2010). The multi-dimensional construct of the six latent exogenous variable shows poor model fit, χ^2 (887) = 2557.176, p = .000 which is statistically significant, indicating an inadequate fit between the covariance matrix of the observed data and the implied covariance matrix of the model.

Other fit indices are also found to hold inadequate values. The GFI = .707, CFI = .691 and TLI = .670 fell below the threshold value of ≥. 90. However, the normed $\chi2/\partial f$ = 2.883 and the RMSEA value = .074 fell between the acceptable range of ≤ 3 and ≤ .08 respectively. Furthermore, the parameter estimates of loading manifest variables of the model ranged from .14 to .88. Loadings should not be below .5 (Byrne, 2010). Thus, the model does not fit the sample data. Figure 7.10 depicts the generated OB multi-dimensional constructs.

The decision was made to drop loadings that were below .5 for better model fit. Therefore, the generated multi-dimensional constructs of OB were re-specified. Out of 12 indicator variables of HA, nine indicators were dropped. Similarly, five indicators were dropped for RR, three were dropped for PS, three were dropped for TC, three were dropped for IM and two were dropped for DL. In total, 25 indicator variables out of 44 were dropped to achieve model fit.

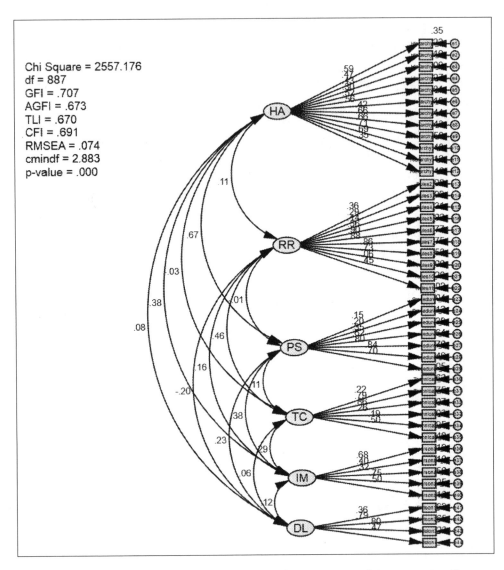

Figure 7.10 Generated Multi-dimensional Constructs of Organizational
Bureaucracy (OB)

Note. HA = Hierarchy of Authority, RR = Rules and Regulation, PS = Procedural Specification,
TC = Technical Competencies, IM = Impersonality and DL = Division of Labor.

The overall re-specified model shows an improved goodness-of-fit indices,
which are consistent with the data. The goodness-of-fit indices of the re-
specified model are substantial. The normed $\chi^2/\partial f$ = 1.961 and the RMSEA
value = .053 fall between the acceptable range of ≤ 3 and ≤ .08 respectively,

which reflects a good fit in the re-specified model. Other fit indices are also found to hold adequate values. The GFI = .927, CFI = .953 and TLI = .942 are above the threshold value of ≥. 90. Table 7.7compares the result of the fit indices of the generated model, the re-specified model against the recommended threshold values.

Table 7.7 Summary of the Fit Indices of the Hypothesized
Multi-dimensional Constructs of OB

Fit Indices	Accepted fit	OB Generated Model	OB Re-specified Model
• Chi-square	Insignificant	2557.176	268.596
• *p* value*	$.001 \leq p \leq .05$	.000	.000
• CMIN/DF	≤ 3	2.883	1.961
• CFI	$\geq .90$	.691	.953
• TLI	$\geq .90$	.670	.942
• GFI	$\geq .90$	.707	.927
• RMSEA	$\leq .08$	.074	.053

Source: Kline (2011); Schumacker and Lomax (1996); Hair et al. (2010); Hu and Bentler (1995); Byrne (2010)
* Statistically significant at .05.

Based on Table 7.7, the re-specified model of the multi-dimensional constructs of OB fell within the range of the accepted fit indices values thus, indicating an adequate fit between the covariance matrix of the observed data and the implied covariance matrix of the model. In addition, the parameter estimates were also examined and were found to be statistically significant. The loadings range from .550 (*Rules5_1*) to .909 (*Rules 6_1*). They are free from any offending estimates and showed the logical direction. The values of the squared multiple correlations (SMC) ranged from .302 (*Rules5_1*) to .826 (*Rules 6_1*). The SMC indicates how well the observed variables serve as the manifests of the latent variables and provide evidence of the reliability of the indicators investigated (Blunch, 2008). It is worth noting that all values of the SMC for the revised multi-dimensional are above .25. Thus, portraying substantial evidence of the variance in the 19 observed variables of the revised multi-dimensional constructs of OB. Figure 7.11 depicts the re-specified OB multi-dimensional constructs.

Based on Figure 7.11, the re-specified multi-dimensional constructs of OB fit the sample data. Further analysis is required to test the convergent validity of the re-specified model. Table 7.8 summarizes the internal reliability, the factor loadings, the average variance extract (AVE) and the composite reliability (CR) for the re-specified model of OB.

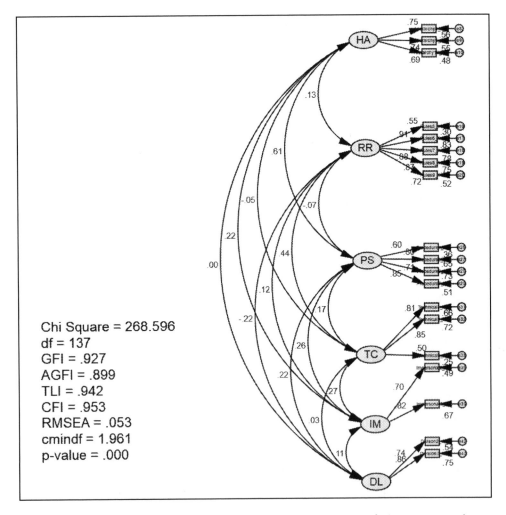

Figure 7.11: Re-specified Multi-dimensional Constructs of Organizational Bureaucracy (OB)

Note. HA = Hierarchy of Authority, RR = Rules and Regulation, PS = Procedural Specification, TC = Technical Competencies, IM = Impersonality and DL = Division of Labor.

From the above table, all constructs have the AVE values ≥ .5 and CR values ≥ .7 respectively. Thus, the re-specified multi-dimensional constructs of OB demonstrated evidence of convergent validity. Based on the fit indices, convergent validity and the internal reliability of the re-specified OB multi-dimensional constructs, the analysis reveals that Hypothesis 2 is supported by the finding that the measurement model of OB is valid and reliable. Thus, Research Question 3 is fully addressed.

Table 7.8 Summary of the Convergent Validity of the Re-specified Multi-dimensional Constructs of OB

Constructs	Items	Internal Reliability (Cronbach Alpha)	Factor Loading	AVE	CR
HA	Hierarchy8_1		.75	.529	.771
	Hierarchy9_1	.771	.74		
	Hierarchy10_1		.69		
RR	Rules5_1		.55		
	Rules6_1		.91		
	Rules7_1	.886	.88	.636	.895
	Rules8_1		.87		
	Rules9_1		.72		
PS	Procedure4_1		.60		
	Procedure5_1	.825	.80	.557	.832
	Procedure6_1		.71		
	Procedure7_1		.85		
TC	Technical4_1		.81		
	Technical5_1	.752	.85	.543	.773
	Technical8_1		.50		
IM	Impersonal2_1	.729	.70	.581	.734
	Impersonal5_1		.82		
DL	Division2_1	.777	.74	.644	.782
	Division3_1		.86		

Note. HA = Hierarchy of Authority, RR = Rules and Regulation, PS = Procedural Specification, TC = Technical Competencies, IM = Impersonality and DL = Division of Labor.

CFA for Multi-Dimensional Constructs of In-Service Training Effectiveness (IST)

The third construct evaluated using CFA belongs to IST. IST consisted of five underlying factors, which were the Participant's Reaction (*Reaction*), Participant's Learning (*Learning*), Organizational Support and Change (*Support*), New Skills and Knowledge (*New*) and Students Learning Outcomes (*Outcomes*). The *reaction* was measured by seven indicator variables. The second factor, *Learning* was measured by five indicator variables. The third factor, *Support* was measured by six indicator variables. The fourth factor, *New* was measured by four indicator variables and the last factor, *Outcomes* was measured by four indicator variables. All 26 items were hypothesized to load on sub-scales of the IST latent constructs. Figure 7.12 depicts the hypothesized IST multi-dimensional constructs.

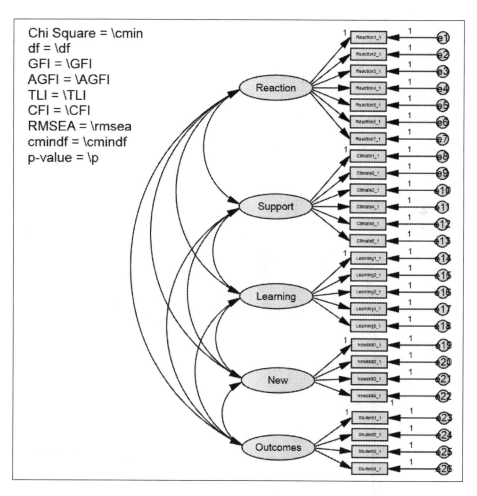

Figure 7.12 Hypothesized Multi-dimensional Constructs of In-Service Training Effectiveness (IST)

Note. Reaction = Participant's Reaction, *Learning* = Participant's Learning, *Support* = Organizational Support and Change, *New* = New Skills and Knowledge and *Outcomes* = Students Learning Outcomes.

The interrelationships among all 26 indicators are statistically significant. The data does not violate the assumption of normality with skewness between ±2 (Tabachnick & Fidell, 2007) and kurtosis between ±7 (Byrne, 2010). The multi-dimensional construct of the five latent exogenous variable shows a poor model fit, χ^2 (289) = 786.985, p = .000 which is statistically significant, indicating an inadequate fit between the covariance matrix of the observed data and the implied covariance matrix of the model.

Other fit indices are also found to hold inadequate values. The CFI = .876 and TLI = .860 fall below the threshold value of ≥ .90. However, the normed $\chi^2/\partial f$ = 2.723 and the RMSEA value = .071 fall between the acceptable range of ≤ 3 and ≤ .08 respectively. Furthermore, the parameter estimates of loading manifest variables of the model ranged from .41 to .83. Loadings should not be below .5 (Byrne, 2010). Thus, the model does not fit the sample data. Figure 7.13 depicts the generated IST multi-dimensional constructs.

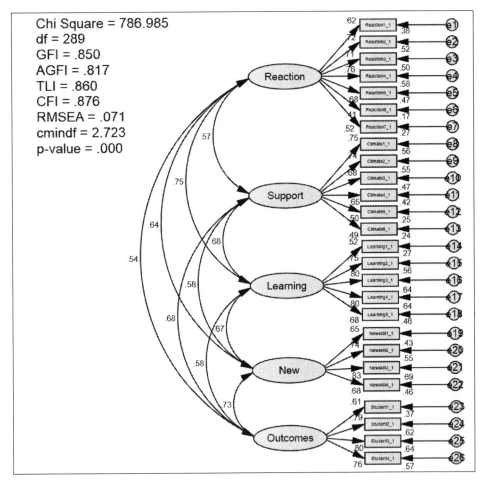

Figure 7.13 Generated Multi-dimensional Constructs of In-Service Training Effectiveness (IST)

Note. Reaction = Participant's Reaction, *Learning* = Participant's Learning, *Support* = Organizational Support and Change, *New* = New Skills and Knowledge and *Outcomes* = Students Learning Outcomes.

The decision was made to drop loadings that were below .5 for better model fit. Therefore, the generated of multi-dimensional constructs of IST were re-specified. Out of seven indicator variables of *Reaction*, were dropped. Similarly, two indicators were dropped for *Support*. No items were dropped from *Learning*, *New* and *Outcomes*. In total, four indicator variables out of 26 were dropped to achieve model fit.

The overall re-specified model shows an improved goodness-of-fit indices, which are consistent with the data. The goodness-of-fit indices of the re-specified model are substantial. The normed $\chi^2/\partial f = 2.398$ and the RMSEA value = .064 fall between the acceptable range of ≤ 3 and $\leq .08$ respectively, which reflected a good fit in the revised model. Other fit indices are also found to hold adequate values. The CFI = .921 and TLI = .908 are above the threshold value of $\geq. 90$. Table 7.9 compares the result of the fit indices of the generated model, the re-specified model against the recommended threshold values.

Table 7.9 Summary of the Fit Indices of the Multi-dimensional Constructs of IST

Fit Indices	Accepted fit	IST Generated Model	IST Re-specified Model
• Chi-square	Insignificant	786.985	477.178
• *p* value*	$.001 \leq p \leq .05$	.000	.000
• CMIN/DF	≤ 3	2.723	2.398
• CFI	$\geq .90$	.876	.921
• TLI	$\geq .90$	.860	.908
• GFI	$\geq .90$	.850	.889
• RMSEA	$\leq .08$	.071	.064

Source: Kline (2011); Schumacker and Lomax (1996); Hair et al. (2010); Hu and Bentler (1995); Byrne (2010)
* Statistically significant at .05.

Based on Table 7.9, the re-specified model of the multi-dimensional constructs of IST fall within the range of the accepted fit indices values thus, indicating an adequate fit between the covariance matrix of the observed data and the implied covariance matrix of the model. In addition, the parameter estimates are also examined and are found to be statistically significant. The loadings range from .514 (*Learning1_1*) to .833 (*Newskill3_1*). They are free from any offending estimates and show the logical direction. The values of the squared multiple correlations (SMC) range from .265 (*Learning1_1*) to .693 (*Newskill3_1*). The SMC indicates how well the observed variables serve as the manifests of the latent variables and provide evidence of the reliability of the indicators investigated (Blunch, 2008). It is worth noting that all values of the SMC for the revised multi-dimensional are above .25.Thus, portraying substantial evidence of the variance in the 22 observed variables of the re-specified multi-dimensional constructs of IST. Figure 7.14 depicts the re-specified IST multi-dimensional constructs.

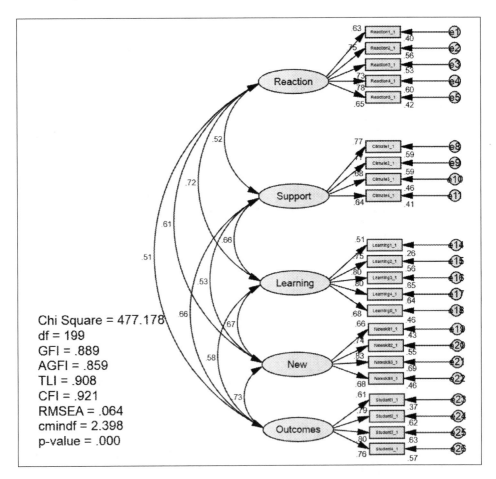

Figure 7.14 Re-specified Multi-dimensional Constructs of In-Service Training Effectiveness (IST)

Note. Reaction = Participant's Reaction, *Learning* = Participant's Learning, *Support* = Organizational Support and Change, *New* = New Skills and Knowledge and *Outcomes* = Students Learning Outcomes.

Based on Figure 7.14, the re-specified multi-dimensional constructs of IST fit the sample data. Further analysis is required to test the convergent validity of the hypothesized model. Table 7.10 summarizes the internal reliability, the factor loadings, the average variance extract (AVE) and the composite reliability (CR) for the re-specified model of IST.

Table 7.10. Summary of the Convergent Validity of the Re-specified Multi-dimensional Constructs of IST

Constructs	Items	Internal Reliability (Cronbach Alpha)	Factor Loading	AVE	CR
Reaction	Reaction1_1		.63		
	Reaction2_1		.75		
	Reaction3_1	.829	.73	.505	.835
	Reaction4_1		.78		
	Reaction5_1		.65		
Support	Climate1_1		.77		
	Climate2_1		.77		
	Climate3_1	.803	.68	.514	.808
	Climate4_1		.64		
	Climate4_1		.80		
Learning	Learning1_1		.51		
	Learning2_1		.75		
	Learning3_1	.823	.80	.513	.837
	Learning4_1		.80		
	Learning5_1		.68		
New	Newskill1_1		.66		
	Newskill2_1	.813	.74	.534	.819
	Newskill3_1		.83		
	Newskill4_1		.68		
Outcomes	Student1_1		.61		
	Student2_1	.820	.79	.553	.831
	Student3_1		.80		
	Student4_1		.76		

Note. *Reaction* = Participant's Reaction, *Learning* = Participant's Learning, *Support* = Organizational Support and Change, *New* = New Skills and Knowledge and *Outcomes* = Students Learning Outcomes.

From the above table, all the constructs have AVE values ≥ .5 and CR values ≥ .7 respectively. Thus, the re-specified hypothesized multi-dimensional constructs of IST has the evidence of convergent validity. Based on the fit indices and the convergent validity of the re-specified hypothesized IST multi-dimensional constructs, the analysis reveals that Hypothesis 3 is supported by the finding that the measurement model of IST is valid and reliable. Thus, Research Question 4 is fully addressed.

CFA for Multi-Dimensional Constructs of Student's Aspiration Outcomes (SA)

The fourth and the last constructs evaluated using CFA belong to SA. SA consisted of six underlying factors which are the Bilingual Proficiency (BP), Knowledge (*Know*), Leadership Skills (*Leader*), National Identity (ID), Thinking Skills (*Think*) and Ethics and Spirituality (*Ethics*). BP was measured by ten indicator variables. The second factor, *Know* was measured by eight indicator variables. The third factor, *Leader* was measured by eight indicator variables. The fourth factor, ID was measured by six indicator variables and the fifth and sixth factor, *Think* and *Ethics* were measured with five and four indicator variables, respectively. All 41 items were hypothesized to load on sub-scales of the SA latent constructs. Figure 7.15 depicts the hypothesized SA multi-dimensional constructs.

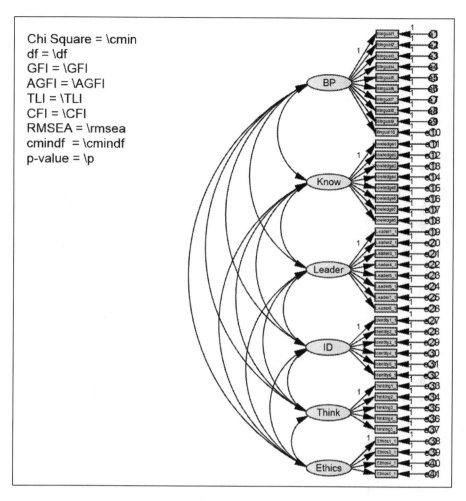

Figure 7.15 Hypothesized Multi-dimensional Constructs of Students'
Aspiration Outcomes (SA)

Note. BP = Bilingual Proficiency, *Know* = Knowledge, *Leader* = Leadership Skills, ID =
National Identity, *Think* = Thinking Skills and *Ethics* = Ethics and Spirituality.

The interrelationships among all 41 indicators are statistically significant.
The data does not violate the assumption of normality with skewness between
±2 (Tabachnick & Fidell, 2007) and kurtosis between ±7 (Byrne, 2010). The
multi-dimensional construct of the six latent exogenous variables show poor
model fit, χ^2 (764) = 2918.846, p = .000 which are statistically significant,
indicating an inadequate fit between the covariance matrix of the observed
data and the implied covariance matrix of the model.

Other fit indices are also found to hold inadequate values. The GFI = .676, CFI = .671 and TLI = .647 fall below the threshold value of ≥. 90. The normed $\chi^2/\partial f$ = 3.820 and the RMSEA value = .091 are out of the acceptable range of ≤ 3 and ≤ .08 respectively. Furthermore, the parameter estimate of loading manifest variables of the model ranged from .310 to .893. Loadings should not be below .5 (Byrne, 2010). Thus, the model does not fit the sample data. Figure 7.16 depicts the generated SA multi-dimensional constructs.

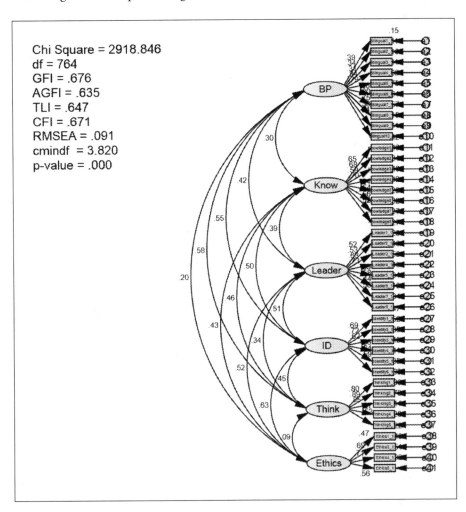

Figure 7.16 Generated Multi-dimensional Constructs of Students' Aspiration Outcomes (SA)

Note. BP = Bilingual Proficiency, *Know* = Knowledge, *Leader* = Leadership Skills, ID = National Identity, *Think* = Thinking Skills and *Ethics* = Ethics and Spirituality.

The decision was made to drop loadings that were below .5 for better model fit. Therefore, the generated multi-dimensional constructs of SA were re-specified. Out of ten indicator variables of BP, six indicators were dropped. Similarly, five indicators were dropped for *Know*, six were dropped for *Leader*, three were dropped for ID, two were dropped for *Think* and two were dropped for *Ethics*. In total, 24 indicator variables out of 41 were dropped to achieve model fit.

The overall re-specified model shows an improved goodness-of-fit indices, which are consistent with the data. The goodness-of-fit indices of the re-specified model are substantial. The normed $\chi^2/\partial f$ = 1.981 and the RMSEA value = .054 fall between the acceptable range of ≤ 3 and ≤ .08 respectively, which reflect a good fit in the revised model. Other fit indices are also found to hold adequate values. The GFI = .932, CFI = .953 and TLI = .954 are above the threshold value of ≥. 90. Table 7.11 compares the result of the fit indices of the generated model, the re-specified model against the recommended threshold values.

Table 7.11. Summary of the Fit Indices of the
Multi-dimensional Constructs of SA

Fit Indices	Accepted fit	SA Generated Model	SA Re-specified Model
• Chi-square	Insignificant	2918.846	206.017
• *p* value*	.001 ≤ *p* ≤.05	.000	.000
• CMIN/DF	≤ 3	3.820	1.961
• CFI	≥ .90	.671	.965
• TLI	≥ .90	.647	.954
• GFI	≥ .90	.676	.932
• RMSEA	≤ .08	.091	.054

Source:Kline (2011); Schumacker and Lomax (1996); Hair et al. (2010); Hu and Bentler (1995); Byrne (2010)
* Statistically significant at .05.

Based on Table 7.11, the re-specified model of the multi-dimensional constructs of SA fell within the range of the accepted fit indices values thus, indicating an adequate fit between the covariance matrix of the observed data and the implied covariance matrix of the model. In addition, the parameter estimates are also examined and are found to be statistically significant. The loadings ranged from .508 (*Identity4_1*) to .952 (*Knowledge7_1*). They are free from any offending estimates and show the logical direction. The values of the squared multiple correlations (SMC) range from .258 (*Identity4_1*) to .907 (*Knowledge7_1*). The SMC indicates how well the observed variables serve as the manifests of the latent variables and provide evidence of the reliability of the indicators investigated (Blunch, 2008). It is worth noting that all values of the SMC for the re-specified multi-dimensional are above .25. Thus, portraying substantial evidence of the variance in the 17 observed variables of the re-specified multi-dimensional constructs of SA. Figure 7.17 depicts the re-specified SA multi-dimensional constructs.

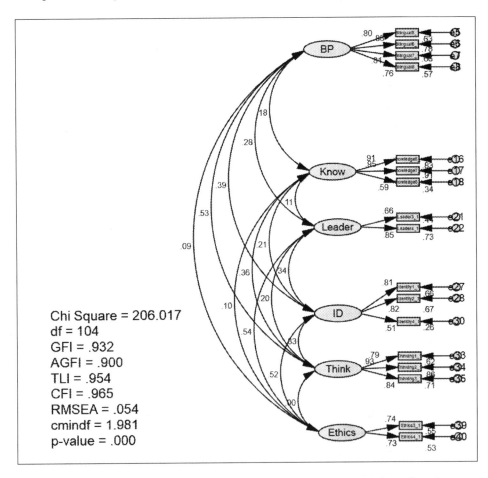

Figure 7.17 Re-specified Multi-dimensional Constructs of Students' Aspiration Outcomes (SA)

Note. BP = Bilingual Proficiency, *Know* = Knowledge, *Leader* = Leadership Skills, ID = National Identity, *Think* = Thinking Skills and *Ethics* = Ethics and Spirituality.

Based on Figure 7.17, the re-specified multi-dimensional constructs of SA fit the sample data. Further analysis is required to test the convergent validity of the re-specified model. Table 7.12 summarizes the internal reliability, the factor loadings, the average variance extract (AVE) and the composite reliability (CR) of the re-specified hypothesized model of SA.

Table 7.12. Summary of the Convergent Validity of the Re-specified Multi-dimensional Constructs of SA

Constructs	Items	Internal Reliability (Cronbach Alpha)	Factor Loading	AVE	CR
BP	Bilingual5_1		.80		
	Bilingual6_1	.883	.88	.662	.887
	Bilingual7_1		.81		
	Bilingual8_1		.76		
Know	Knowledge6_1		.91		
	Knowledge7_1	.848	.95	.693	.867
	Knowledge8_1		.59		
Leader	Leader3_1	.721	.66	.579	.730
	Leader4_1		.85		
ID	Identity1_1		.81		
	Identity2_1	.740	.82	.530	.764
	Identity4_1		.51		
Think	Thinking1_1		.79		
	Thinking2_1	.889	.93	.732	.891
	Thinking3_1		.84		
Ethics	Ethics3_1	.699	.74	.540	.701
	Ethics4_1		.73		

Note. BP = Bilingual Proficiency, Know = Knowledge, Leader = Leadership Skills, ID = National Identity, Think = Thinking Skills and Ethics = Ethics and Spirituality.

From the above table, all the constructs have AVE values ≥ .5 and CR values ≥ .7 respectively. Thus, the re-specified multi-dimensional constructs of SA show evidence of convergent validity. Based on the fit indices and the convergent validity of the re-specified SA multi-dimensional constructs, the analysis reveals that Hypothesis 4 is supported by the finding that the measurement model of SA is valid and reliable. Thus, Research Question 5 is fully addressed.

TECHNICAL AND VOCATIONAL EDUCATION STUDENTS' ASPIRATION INVENTORY (TVESAI)

This subsection discusses in detail the analyses involved in establishing the Technical and Vocational Education Students' Aspirations Inventory (TVESAI). TVESAI is the hypothesized model under study that has been elaborated earlier in Chapter 1 and Chapter 2. The results of the CFA for each variable in subsection 4.5 were used to develop the model. The item parcelling technique was used, to sum up the remaining items for each construct. The technique was used for the purpose of simplifying the framework to the construct level. Thus, the model shows the relationship between the variables based on the constructs. To develop TVESAI, a measurement model and a structural model must first be established.

The Measurement Model of TVESAI
Model Specification

The measurement model of TVESAI consists of four variables with the remaining constructs from the CFA. The first variable is strategic leadership practices (SL) with seven constructs: Strategic Alignment (*first_align*), Strategic Intervention (*first_interven*), Strategic Orientation (*first_orient*), Restlessness (*first_restless*), Absorptive Capacity (*first_absorp*),Adaptive Capacity (*first adapt*) and Wisdom (*first_Wisdom*). The second variable is organizational bureaucracy (OB) with six constructs: Hierarchy of Authority (HA), Rules and Regulation (RR), Procedural Specification (PS), Technical Competencies (TC), Impersonality (IM) and Division of Labor (DL). The third variable is in-service training effectiveness (IST) with five constructs: Participant's Reaction (*Reaction*), Participant's Learning (*Learning*), Organizational Support and Change (*Support*), New Skills and Knowledge (*New*) and = Students Learning Outcomes (*Outcomes*). The last and the fourth variable is students' aspirations which has six constructs: Bilingual Proficiency (BP), Knowledge (*Know*), Leadership Skills (*Leader*), National Identity (ID), Thinking Skills (*Think*) and Ethics and Spirituality (*Ethics*). Figure 7.18 depicts the hypothesized measurement model of TVESAI.

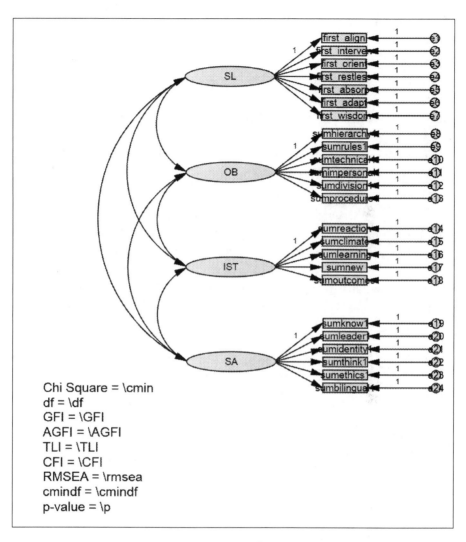

Figure 7.18 Hypothesized Measurement Model of TVESAI

Note. SL = Strategic Leadership Practices, *first_align* = Strategic Alignment, *first_interven* = Strategic Intervention, *first_orient* = Strategic Orientation, *first_restless* = Restlessness, *first_absorp* = Absorptive Capacity, *first adapt* = Adaptive Capacity, *first_Wisdom* = Wisdom, OB = Organizational Bureaucracy, *sumhierarchy1* = Hierarchy of Authority, *sumrules1* = Rules and Regulation, *sumprocedure1* = Procedural Specification, *sumtechnical1* = Technical Competencies, *sumimpersonal1* = Impersonality, sumdivision1 = Division of Labor, IST = In-service Training Effectiveness, *sumreaction* = Participant's Reaction, *sumlearning* = Participant's Learning, *sumclimate* = Organizational Support and Change, *sumnew* = New Skills and Knowledge, *sumoutcomes* = Students Learning Outcomes, SA = Students' Aspiration Outcomes, *sumbilingual1* = Bilingual Proficiency, *sumknow1* = Knowledge, *sumleader1* = Leadership Skills, *sumidentity1* = National Identity, *sumthink1* = Thinking Skills and *sumethics1* = Ethics and Spirituality.

Model Estimation

The interrelationships among all 24 constructs are statistically significant except for *sumrules1* and *sumtechnical1*. Data does not violate the assumption of normality with skewness between ±2 (Tabachnick & Fidell, 2007) and kurtosis between ±7 (Byrne, 2010). The measurement model shows poor model fit, χ^2 (246) = 988.639, p = .000 which is statistically significant, indicating an inadequate fit between the covariance matrix of the observed data and the implied covariance matrix of the model.

Other fit indices are also found to hold inadequate values. The GFI = .778, CFI = .753 and TLI = .723 fall below the threshold value of ≥. 90. The normed $\chi^2/\partial f$ = 4.019 and the RMSEA value = .094 are out of the acceptable range of ≤ 3 and ≤ .08 respectively. Furthermore, the parameter estimates range from -.06 to 1.18. The loadings should not be below .5 and not more than 1 (Byrne, 2010). In addition, the data set exhibits signs of multivariate outliers. Thus, the model does not fit the sample data. Figure 7.19 depicts the generated measurement model of TVESAI.

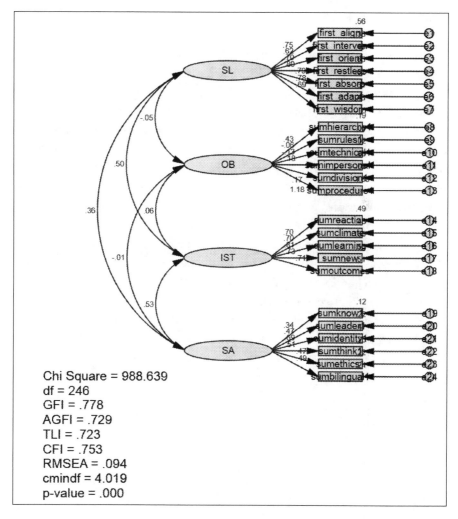

Figure 7.19 Generated Measurement Model of TVESAI

Note. SL = Strategic Leadership Practices, *first_align* = Strategic Alignment, *first_interven* = Strategic Intervention, *first_orient* = Strategic Orientation, *first_restless* = Restlessness, *first_absorp* = Absorptive Capacity, *first adapt* = Adaptive Capacity, *first_Wisdom* = Wisdom, OB = Organizational Bureaucracy, *sumhierarchy1* = Hierarchy of Authority, *sumrules1* = Rules and Regulation, *sumprocedure1* = Procedural Specification, *sumtechnical1* = Technical Competencies, *sumimpersonal1* = Impersonality, sumdivision1 = Division of Labor, IST = In-service Training Effectiveness, *sumreaction* = Participant's Reaction, *sumlearning* = Participant's Learning, *sumclimate* = Organizational Support and Change, *sumnew* = New Skills and Knowledge, *sumoutcomes* = Students Learning Outcomes, SA = Students' Aspiration Outcomes, *sumbilingual1* = Bilingual Proficiency, *sumknow1* = Knowledge, *sumleader1* = Leadership Skills, *sumidentity1* = National Identity, *sumthink1* = Thinking Skills and *sumethics1* = Ethics and Spirituality.

Model Re-specification

Firstly, four cases of multivariate outliers were dropped from the dataset; Respondents 26, 195, 271 and 293, leaving the sampled data final total of 339. Secondly, the decision was made to drop loadings that were below .5 and more than 1 for better model fit. Therefore, the generated measurement model of TVESAI was re-specified. Out of six constructs of OB, four were dropped. Similarly, three constructs were dropped for SA. In total, seven constructs out of 24 were dropped to achieve model fit. Following this, two inter-correlation between four errors were freed based on the suggestions of MIs; the connection between error 5 (*first_orient*) and error 7 (*first_align*) and error 17 (*sumnew*) and error 18 (*sumoutcome*).

The overall re-specified model shows improved goodness-of-fit indices, whichare consistent with the data. The goodness-of-fit indices of the re-specified model are substantial. The normed $\chi^2/\partial f$ = 2.145 and the RMSEA value = .058 fall between the acceptable range of ≤ 3 and $\leq .08$ respectively, which reflect a good fit in the revised model. Other fit indices are also found to hold adequate values. The GFI = .919, CFI = .951 and TLI = .940 are above the threshold value of $\geq$. 90. Table 7.13 compares the result of the fit indices of the generated model, the re-specified model against the recommended threshold values.

Table 7.13. Summary of the Fit Indices of the
Measurement Model of TVESAI

Fit Indices	Accepted fit	Generated Model	Re-specified Model
• Chi-square	Insignificant	988.639	238. 053
• *p* value*	$.001 \leq p \leq .05$	.000	.000
• CMIN/DF	≤ 3	4.019	2.145
• CFI	$\geq .90$	.753	.951
• TLI	$\geq .90$	.723	.940
• GFI	$\geq .90$	.778	.919
• RMSEA	$\leq .08$	.094	.058

Source: Kline (2011); Schumacker and Lomax (1996); Hair et al. (2010); Hu and Bentler (1995); Byrne (2010)
* Statistically significant at .05.

Based on Table 7.13, the re-specified model fall within the range of the accepted fit indices values thus, indicating an adequate fit between the covariance matrix of the observed data and the implied covariance matrix of the model. In addition, the parameter estimates are also examined and are found to be statistically significant. The loadings range from .519 (*sumleader1*) to .847 (*sumlearning*). They are free from any offending estimates and showed the logical direction. The values of the squared multiple correlations (SMC) range from .269 (*sumleader1*) to .717 (*sumlearning*). The SMC indicates how well the observed variables serve as the manifests of the latent variables and provide evidence of the reliability of the indicators investigated (Blunch, 2008). It is worth noting that all values of the SMC for the re-specified multi-dimensional are above .25. Thus, portraying substantial evidence of the variance in the 17 observed variables of the re-specified measurement model of TVESAI. Figure 7.20 depicts the re-specified measurement model of TVESAI.

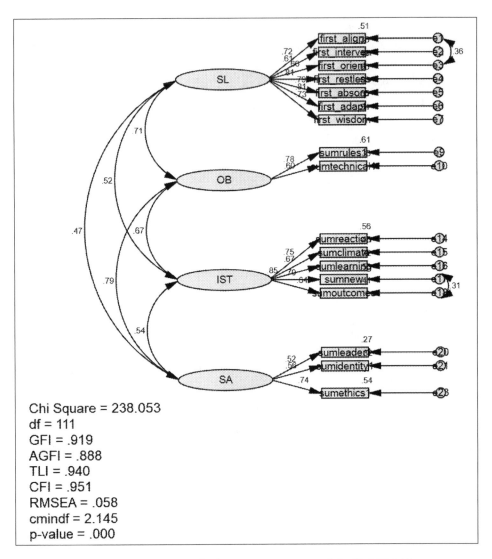

Figure 7.20 Re-specified Measurement Model of TVESAI

Note. SL = Strategic Leadership Practices, *first_align* = Strategic Alignment, *first_interven* = Strategic Intervention, *first_orient* = Strategic Orientation, *first_restless* = Restlessness, *first_absorp* = Absorptive Capacity, *first adapt* = Adaptive Capacity, *first_Wisdom* = Wisdom, OB = Organizational Bureaucracy, *sumrules1* = Rules and Regulation, *sumtechnical1* = Technical Competencies, IST = In-service Training Effectiveness, *sumreaction* = Participant's Reaction, *sumlearning* = Participant's Learning, *sumclimate* = Organizational Support and Change, *sumnew* = New Skills and Knowledge, *sumoutcomes* = Students Learning Outcomes, SA = Students' Aspiration Outcomes, *sumleader1* = Leadership Skills, *sumidentity1* = National Identity and *sumethics1* = Ethics and Spirituality.

Based on Figure 7.20 the re-specified measurement model of TVESAI fits the sample data. Further analysis is required to test the discriminant validity of the re-specified measurement model. Table 7.14 summarizes the squared correlations and the average variance extract (AVE) of the re-specified measurement model.

Table 7.14. Summary of the AVE and the Squared
Correlations of the Re-specified Measurement Model

	SL	OB	IST	SA
SL	**0.5430**			
OB	0.5013	**0.4870**		
IST	0.2663	0.4422	**0.5280**	
SA	0.2256	0.6241	0.2905	**0.3760**

Note. Diagonals represent the average variance extracted while the other entries represent the squared correlations

To demonstrate discriminant validity, the AVE of one construct should be larger than the squared correlations between the variables. Based on Table 7.14, all constructs fulfilled the discriminant validity except for squared correlations values of SL – OB and OB – SA. The variables were further analysed for the structural model of TVESAI.

The Structural Model of TVESAI
Model Specification

The hypothesized structural model of TVESAI comprised of 17 manifest variables (constructs) from four variables. The first variable is strategic leadership practices (SL) with seven constructs: strategic alignment (*first_align*), strategic intervention (*first_interven*), strategic orientation (*first_orient*), restlessness (*first_restless*), absorptive capacity (*first_absorp*), adaptive capacity (*first_adapt*) and wisdom (*first_wisdom*). The second variable is organizational bureaucracy (OB) that consists of two constructs: rules and regulations (*sumrules1*) and technical competencies (*sumtechnical1*). The third variable is in-service training effectiveness (IST), which consists of five constructs: participant's reaction (*sumreaction*), organizational support and change (*sumclimate*), participant's learning (sumlearning), new skills and knowledge (*sumnew*) and student's learning outcomes (*outcomes*). The fourth and the last variable involves in the study is students' aspirations (SA), which consists of three constructs: leadership skills (*sumleader*), national identity (*sumidentity*) and ethics and spirituality (*sumethics*).

The hypothesized model was statistically tested through the same method of CFA and measurement model analysis, i.e. the goodness-of-fit indices (normed $\chi^2/\partial f$, RMSEA, GFI, CFI and TLI). Figure 7.21 presents the hypothesized structural model of TVESAI.

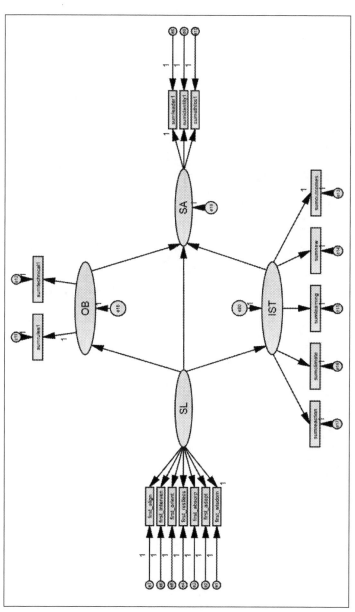

Figure 7.21 The Hypothesized Structural Model of TVESAI

Note. SL = Strategic Leadership Practices, *first_align* = Strategic Alignment, *first_interven* = Strategic Intervention, *first_orient* = Strategic Orientation, *first_restless* = Restlessness, *first_absorp* = Absorptive Capacity, *first_Wisdom* = Wisdom, OB = Organizational Bureaucracy, *sumrules1* = Rules and Regulation, *sumtechnical1* = Technical Competencies, IST = In-service Training Effectiveness, *sumreaction* = Participant's Reaction, *sumlearning* = Participant's Learning, *sumclimate* = Organizational Support and Change, *sumnew* = New Skills and Knowledge, *sumoutcomes* = Students Learning Outcomes, SA = Students' Aspiration Outcomes, *sumleader1* = Leadership Skills, *sumidentity1* = National Identity and *sumethics1* = Ethics and Spirituality.

Model Estimation

The hypothesized structural model was estimated by implementing ML estimation of the data collected from the sample of 339 administrators. The results of the model were evaluated using the goodness-of-fit indices as in the earlier part of the analysis. The inter-variable correlations were assessed and were statistically significant. The correlations, the means and the standard deviation of each construct (summated score) of the hypothesized model are shown in Table 7.14.

The results of the hypothesized structural model exhibit poor fitting values. The χ^2 (114) = 335.671 and p = .000 which are statistically significant, indicating an inadequate fit between the covariance matrix of the observed data and the implied covariance matrix of the model. Other fit indices (specifically GFI = .894 and TLI = .897) are also found to hold inadequate values, which fall below the threshold value of ≥. 90. However, the CFI = .914 (≥. 90), the normed $\chi^2/\partial f$ = 2.944 (≤. 90) and the RMSEA value = .076 (≤. 08) exhibit good fit values.

Table 7.15. Inter-variable correlations, Means and Standard Deviation of the Constructs of the Hypothesized Model

	first_ align	first_ interven	first_ orient	first_ restless	first_ absorp	first_ adapt	first_ wisdom	sumrules1	sumtech -nical1	sum- reaction	sum- climate	sum- learning	sum- new	sum- outcomes	sum- leader1	sum- identity1	sum- ethics1
first_align																	
first_interven	.544**																
first_orient	.661**	.463**															
first_restless	.572**	.512**	.567**														
first_absorp	.605**	.467**	.499**	.616*													
first_adapt	.560**	.458**	.508**	.645**	.691**												
first_wisdom	.470**	.425**	.465**	.628**	.571**	.590**											
sumrules1	.390**	.313**	.361**	.494**	.395**	.473**	.476**										
sumtechnical1	.279**	.180**	.186**	.334**	.291**	.331**	.340**	.470**									
sumreaction	.232**	.192**	.213**	.325**	.328**	.364**	.343**	.456**	.379**								
sumclimate	.238**	.264**	.206**	.272**	.250**	.216**	.144**	.234**	.247**	.463**							
sumlearning	.282**	.283**	.299**	.378**	.361**	.369**	.338**	.424**	.364**	.637**	.588**						
sumnew	.303**	.230**	.268**	.279**	.316**	.297**	.272**	.396**	.328**	.524**	.477**	.591**					
sumoutcomes	.201**	.204**	.141**	.210**	.274**	.202**	.189**	.276**	.204**	.459**	.565**	.513**	.618**				
sumleader1	.198**	.223**	.214**	.222**	.266**	.149**	.196**	.276**	.263**	.237**	.189**	.264**	.237**	.275**			
sumidentity1	.149**	.149**	.256**	.238**	.193**	.127*	.228**	.354**	.276**	.306**	.300**	.279**	.236**	.301**	.260**		
sumethics1	.185**	.200**	.272**	.313**	.252**	.228**	.345**	.466**	.352**	.339**	.136**	.301**	.225**	.165**	.404**	.411**	
Mean	4.11	3.91	4.23	4.30	4.22	4.3	4.43	4.33	4.12	4.11	3.82	4.08	4.04	3.86	3.94	3.87	4.33
SD	0.47	0.51	0.52	0.47	0.46	0.45	0.53	0.45	0.53	0.41	0.45	0.42	0.41	0.45	0.62	0.60	0.58
Alpha	0.812	0.761	0.690	0.776	0.761	0.764	0.917	0.886	0.752	0.829	0.803	0.823	0.813	0.820	0.721	0.740	0.699

Note. N = 339, SD = standard deviation, ** $p \leq .001$ and * $p \leq .05$.

All path coefficients are positively directed with reasonable magnitudes, except the direct path coefficient between SL → SA. The direct path coefficient between SL → SA (-.18) was found to exhibit an offending estimate. However, the direct causal path between OB and SA and IST and SA are both statistically significant. Similarly, the indirect path causal path between SL and SA through OB and SL and SA through IST are also both statistically significant. The hypothesized model must be revised for a better fitting model considering poor values of the fit indices values (GFI and TLI) and the offending estimates between SL → SA. Figure 7.22 depicts the generated structural model of TVESAI.

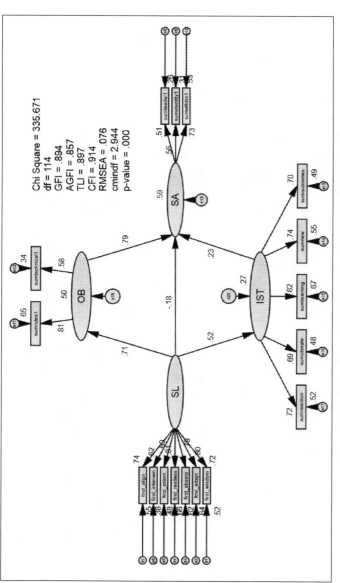

Figure 7.22 The Generated Structural Model of TVESAI

Note. SL = Strategic Leadership Practices, *first_align* = Strategic Alignment, *first_interven* = Strategic Intervention, *first_orient* = Strategic Orientation, *first_restless* = Restlessness, *first_absorp* = Absorptive Capacity, *first adapt* = Adaptive Capacity, *first_Wisdom* = Wisdom, OB = Organizational Bureaucracy, *sumrules1* = Rules and Regulation, *sumtechnical1* = Technical Competencies, IST = In-service Training Effectiveness, *sumreaction* = Participant's Reaction, *sumlearning* = Participant's Learning, *sumclimate* = Organizational Support and Change, *sumnew* = New Skills and Knowledge, *sumoutcomes* = Students Learning Outcomes, SA = Students' Aspiration Outcomes, *sumleader1* = Leadership Skills, *sumidentity1* = National Identity and *sumethics1* = Ethics and Spirituality.

Model Re-specification

The aim of the re-specified model is to seek a better fit. Therefore, Post Hoc MIs are investigated in order to identify a more parsimonious model. Firstly, the offending estimate of the direct coefficient of the direct effect of SL → SA is eliminated from the model due to exhibiting an illogical order. Following this, one inter-correlation between two errors was freed based on the suggestions of MIs; the connection between error 5 (*first_orient*) and error 7 (*first_align*). The co-varied connection reduce the χ^2 value from 335.671 (generated model) to 297.151 (re-specified model), thus increasing the fit indices. Theoretically, two correlated measurement errors showing a proof of communalities among pairs of manifest variables are involved.

The overall re-specified model shows improved goodness-of-fit indices, which are consistent with the data. The goodness-of-fit indices of the re-specified model are substantial. The normed $\chi^2/\partial f = 2.607$ and the RMSEA value = .069 fall between the acceptable range of ≤ 3 and ≤ .08 respectively, which reflect good fit in the re-specified model. Other fit indices are also found to hold adequate values. The GFI = .905, CFI = .929 and TLI = .915 are above the threshold value of ≥. 90. Table 7.15 compares the result of the fit indices of the generated model, the re-specified model against the recommended threshold values.

Table 7.16. Summary of the Fit Indices of the Structural Model of TVESAI

Fit Indices	Accepted fit	Generated Model	Re-specified Model
• Chi-square	Insignificant	335.671	297.151
• *p* value*	.001 ≤ *p* ≤.05	.000	.000
• CMIN/DF	≤ 3	2.944	2.607
• CFI	≥ .90	.914	.929
• TLI	≥ .90	.897	.915
• GFI	≥ .90	.894	.905
• RMSEA	≤ .08	.076	.069

Source:Kline (2011); Schumacker and Lomax (1996); Hair et al. (2010); Hu and Bentler (1995); Byrne (2010)
* Statistically significant at .05.

In addition, an examination of the parameter estimates is found to be statistically significant. The loadings ranged from .516 (*sumleader1*) to .833

(*sumrules1*). They are free from any offending estimate and showed logical direction. Similarly, the SMC values for the re-specified model fulfilled the requirement of .25 or greater for all indicators. The values ranged from .267 (*sumleader1*) to .694 (*sumrules1*). This provided substantial values in explaining the variance of the 17 constructs (summated) of the re-specified structural model of TVESAI. Figure 7.23 depicts the re-specified structural model of TVESAI.

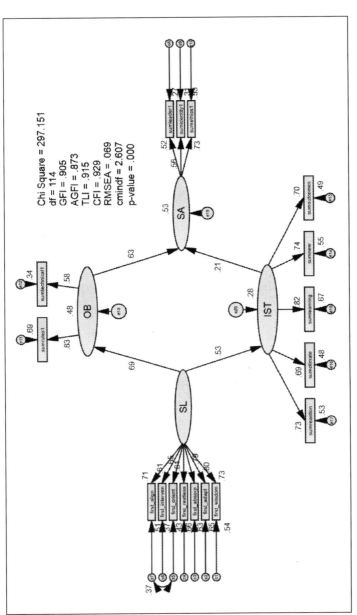

Figure 7.23 The Re-specified Structural Model of TVESAI

Note. SL = Strategic Leadership Practices, *first_align* = Strategic Alignment, *first_interven* = Strategic Intervention, *first_orient* = Strategic Orientation, *first_restless* = Restlessness, *first_absorp* = Absorptive Capacity, *first_adapt* = Adaptive Capacity, *first_Wisdom* = Wisdom, OB = Organizational Bureaucracy, *sumrules1* = Rules and Regulation, *sumtechnical1* = Technical Competencies, IST = In-service Training Effectiveness, *sumreaction* = Participant's Reaction, *sumlearning* = Participant's Learning, *sumclimate* = Organizational Support and Change, *sumnew* = New Skills and Knowledge, *sumoutcomes* = Students Learning Outcomes, SA = Students' Aspiration Outcomes, *sumleader1* = Leadership Skills, *sumidentity1* = National Identity and *sumethics1* = Ethics and Spirituality.

Testing the Directional Effects among the Variables of the Study

This subsection answers the research questions of the direct relationship between SL and SA, OB and SA, IST and SA by testing the three hypotheses below:

1. **RQ$_6$**: Is there a direct and significant relationship between SL and SA?
   H$_5$: There is a direct and significant relationship between SL and SA.
2. **RQ$_7$**: Is there a direct and significant relationship between OB and SA?
   H$_6$: There is a direct and significant relationship between OB and SA.
3. **RQ$_8$**: Is there a direct and significant relationship between IST and SA?
   H$_7$: There is a direct and significant relationship between IST and SA.

To answer each research question, each hypothesis must be tested. For the hypothesis to be supported, the relationship between the variables should be significant at $p = .05$ (C.R >1.96) followed by a logical direct causal effect between the variables.

For RQ$_6$ and H$_5$, the direct path coefficient between SL $\rightarrow$ SA was statistically insignificant. In addition, the negative direct effect demonstrates illogical direct causal effect between SL $\rightarrow$ SA (*see* Figure 4.22). As a result, the direction was dropped for further analysis since it exhibited an illogical causal effect. Hence, there is no direct and significant relationship between SL and SA outcomes and H$_5$ is not supported. Consequently, answering RQ$_6$, there is no direct and significant relationship between SL and SA outcomes.

Secondly, the relationship between OB and SA was investigated to answer RQ$_7$ and to see whether H$_6$ is supported or otherwise. Based on Figure 4.23, the direct path coefficient between OB $\rightarrow$ SA was relatively high and statistically significant (.63). The result indicates that OB substantially determined the SA construct. Hence, there is a direct and significant relationship between OB and SA outcomes, and H$_6$ is supported. Consequently, answering RQ$_7$, there is a direct and significant relationship between OB and SA outcomes.

Thirdly, the relationship between IST and SA was investigated to answer RQ$_8$ and to see whether H$_7$ is supported or otherwise. Based on Figure 4.23, the direct path coefficient between IST $\rightarrow$ SA was relatively low but statistically significant (.21). The result indicates that IST substantially determined the SA construct. Hence, there is a direct and significant relationship between IST and SA outcomes, and H$_7$ is supported. Consequently, answering RQ$_8$, there is a direct and significant relationship between IST and SA outcomes.

Testing the Indirectional Effects among the Variables of the Study

This subsection answers the research questions of the indirect relationship between SL and SA, OB and SA, IST and SA by testing the two hypotheses below:

1. **RQ$_9$**: Does OB mediate the relationship between SL and SA?
   H$_8$:OB mediates the relationship between SL and SA.
2. **RQ$_{10}$**:Does IST mediate the relationship between SL and SA?
   H$_9$:IST mediates the relationship between SL and SA.

According to Kline (2011), the significance of the indirect effect between two variables holds if the standardised direct effect value from one variable to another variable, through a variable is more than .08 and vice versa.

Given the aforementioned formula by Kline (2011), the magnitude of the indirect effect of SL on SA through OB was assessed. The calculation reveals that the value was far greater than .08 (.69 x .63 = .4347). This result indicates that SL significantly affects SA indirectly through OB. Hence, OB mediates the relationship between SL and SA and H$_8$ is supported. Consequently, RQ$_9$ is fully addressed.

Consequently, the magnitude of the indirect effect of SL on SA through IST was assessed. The calculation reveals that the value was greater than .08 (.53 x .21 = .1113). This result indicates that SL significantly affects SA indirectly through IST. Hence, IST mediates the relationship between SL and SA and H$_9$ is supported. Consequently, RQ$_{10}$ is fully addressed. Table 7.16 summarizes the direct and indirect effects of the structural model of TVESAI.

Table 7.17. The Direct and Indirect Effects of TVESAI

Parameters	Standardised Estimates	Critical Ratios (C.R)
Direct Effects		
• SL → SA	-	-
• OB → SA	.628	5.869
• IST → SA	.211	2.868
Indirect Effects		
• SL → OB → SA	.4347	-
• SL → IST → SA	.1113	-

Comparison of the Re-specified TVESAI Model with Alternative Models

This subsection addresses the following research question and hypothesis:

RQ$_{11}$:Is the revised hypothesized structural equation model of TVESAI valid and reliable?

H$_{10}$:The revised hypothesized structural equation model of TVESAI is valid and reliable.

To test the hypothesis, other competing models were established to compare the usefulness of the TVESAI model or otherwise. The first competing model fixed the causal relationship between OB $\rightarrow$ SA and IST $\rightarrow$ SA at zero. The second competing model constrained the relationship between SL $\rightarrow$ SA at zero but was dropped since its logical causal direct relationship was not supported in the generated TVESAI model. As such, only the TVESAI model and the first competing model were examined.

The first competing model exhibited poor fitting values. The χ^2 (116) = 398.663 and p = .000 which were statistically significant, indicating an inadequate fit between the covariance matrix of the observed data and the implied covariance matrix of the model. Other fit indices (GFI = .874 and TLI = .871, CFI = .890) were also found to hold inadequate values which fell below the threshold value of $\geq$. 90. In addition, the normed $\chi^2/\partial f$ = 3.437 ($\leq$. 3) and the RMSEA value = .085 ($\leq$. 08) exhibited poor fit values.

In a nutshell, the TVESAI model shows the best fit indices in comparison with the first competing model. The forgoing results led to addressing H$_{10}$ with the findings that the revised structural equation model (TVESAI model) is valid and reliable. Thus, RQ$_{11}$ is fullyaddressed. Table 7.17 compares the result of the fit indices of the TVESAI, the competing model against the recommended threshold values.

Table 7.18. Summary of the Fit Indices of the
TVESAI and the Competing Model

Fit Indices	Accepted fit	Competing Model	Re-specified Model
• Chi-square	Insignificant	398.663	297.151
• *p* value*	.001 ≤ *p* ≤.05	.000	.000
• CMIN/DF	≤ 3	3.437	2.607
• CFI	≥ .90	.890	.929
• TLI	≥ .90	.871	.915
• GFI	≥ .90	.874	.905
• RMSEA	≤ .08	.076	.069

Source: Kline (2011); Schumacker and Lomax (1996); Hair et al. (2010); Hu and Bentler (1995); Byrne (2010)
* Statistically significant at .05.

Thus far, all 11 research questions have been addressed by testing the research hypotheses. Table 7.18 summarizes the results of the main findings of the study. The discussion of the findings will be presented in Chapter Eight.

Table 7.19. Summary of the Main Findings of the Study

Hypotheses	Findings
H_1: The strategic leadership practices measurement model is valid and reliable.	Supported
H_2: The organizational bureaucracy measurement model is valid and reliable.	Supported
H_3: The in-service training effectiveness measurement model is valid and reliable.	Supported
H_4: The students' aspiration outcomes measurement model is valid and reliable.	Supported
H_5: There is a direct and significant relationship between strategic leadership practices and students' aspiration outcomes.	Not supported*
H_6: There is a direct and significant relationship between organizational bureaucracy and students' aspiration outcomes.	Supported

Hypotheses	Findings
H₇: There is a direct and significant relationship between in-service training effectiveness and students' aspiration outcomes.	Supported
H₈: Organizational bureaucracy mediates the relationship between strategic leadership practices and students' aspiration outcomes.	*Supported*
H₉: In-service training effectiveness mediates the relationship between strategic leadership practices and students' aspiration outcomes.	Supported
H₁₀: The revised hypothesized structural equation model of the TVESAI is valid and reliable.	*Supported*

Chapter seven deliberated the findings of the study, presenting the descriptive analysis of the sampled data, primarily the demographic profiles of the respondents and the descriptive analysis of the variables. It then focuses on the test of statistical assumptions for SEM, followed by the research findings according to the research questions. The study, as highlighted in this chapter, found significant relationships between OB ⇒ SA and IST ⇒ SA and also, both OB and IST mediate the relationship between SL and SA. The following chapter discusses the findings.

CHAPTER EIGHT

THE STRATEGIC LEADERSHIP PRACTICES OF VOCATIONAL COLLEGE LEADERS: THE WAY FORWARD

INTRODUCTION

This chapter summarizes and discusses the results of the study. It begins with a discussion of the findings of the research hypotheses, structured by the research objectives. This followed by the pattern of the descriptive statistics, the final multi-dimensional constructs of each variable: SL, OB, IST and SA, and the direct and indirect relationships among the four variables as depicted in the Technical and Vocational Education Student's Aspiration Inventory (TVESAI). The chapter proceeds by presenting the theoretical and practical implications of the research to the respective body of knowledge and the Malaysian government agencies, respectively. This is then followed by recommendations for future research. The final subsection concludes the whole research.

DISCUSSION OF FINDINGS

The main objective of this research is to explore the causal relationships among SL, OB, IST and SA about the Malaysian Technical and Vocational Education. The study hypothesized that there are causal relationships among

SL, OB, and IST on SA. The use of basic and advanced statistical analyzes screened the data, tested the hypotheses and answered all research questions.

The Level of Strategic Leadership Practices (SL), Organizational Bureaucracy (OB), In-Service Training Effectiveness (IST) and Students' Aspiration Outcomes (SA)

In terms of strategic leadership practices, the results show that vocational college leaders possessed high organizational capabilities, i.e. strategic orientation, strategic competencies, strategic alignment, strategic translation and strategic intervention. The highest organizational capability is strategic orientation ($M = 4.184$, $SD = .4578$) and the lowest organizational capability is strategic intervention ($M = 3.930$, $SD = .4716$). The vocational college leaders also possessed high individual characteristics, i.e. restlessness, wisdom, adaptive capacity and absorptive capacity. The highest characteristic is restlessness ($M = 4.221$, $SD = .4403$) and the lowest individual characteristic is absorptive capacity ($M = 4.129$, $SD = .4366$). In making comparison between organizational capabilities and individual characteristics, the vocational college leaders possessed higher individual characteristics than organizational capabilities traits. The findings are in congruence with those by Adelakun (2015), Nasruddeen (2015), Ali (2013) and Nazifah (2012) who also found a high level of strategic leadership practices among educational leaders. Pisapia et al. (2009) also concluded that despite the Eastern and Western cultural norms, educational leaders practice elements of strategic leadership in managing their schools.

As for OB, the results show moderate to high levels of OB at their schools. The highest level of OB occurred in the aspect of rules and regulations ($M = 4.147$, $SD = .3811$), followed by technical competencies and impersonality while the level of OB for the division of labour, the hierarchy of authority and procedural specification were moderate. The lowest score among the three scores was the division of labour ($M = 2.358$, $SD = .7950$). Thus, the level of OB in the vocational colleges varied from moderate to high depending on the organizational aspect. The findings are supported by other scholars who observed the similar variation of OB level ranging from moderate to high among educational leaders (Ristapawa & Mohd, 2014; Kutlu & Polat, 2011; Yucel, 1999).

As for IST, the study measured the effectiveness of courses attended by vocational college leaders for the past two years. Based on the research findings, it can be concluded that the courses attended by the vocational college leaders were highly effective in terms of the participants' reaction, participants' learning, participants' use of new knowledge and skills, students' learning outcomes and organization support and change. The highest score is participant's learning ($M = 4.075$, $SD = .3818$) and participant's reaction ($M = 4.075$, $SD = .4217$) and the lowest score was in the aspect of organization support and change ($M = 3.826$, $SD = .4189$). Thus, the level of IST effectiveness as perceived by the vocational college leaders varied from moderate to high depending on the organizational aspect. Thus, it can be assumed that the in-service training was beneficial to the vocational college leaders. On the contrary, Uysal (2012), and Azam and Zainurin (2011) concluded a mixed perception (varies from low to high) of school teachers on their in-service training programmes. Hence, based on the different perceptions of IST effectiveness, it can be concluded that IST operationalization varies across educational institutions.

The study also measured the current level of SA from the vocational leaders' perspective. The findings indicate that the level of SA of the vocational college students was high. Vocational college students possessed all six attributes of student aspirations; ethics and spirituality, knowledge, national identity, leadership skills, bilingual proficiency and thinking skills. The highest level of an attribute to SA was ethics and spirituality ($M = 4.209$, $SD = .4991$) while, the lowest level of an attribute to SA was thinking skills ($M = 3.412$, $SD = .6745$). Hence, the vocational college students had high levels of SA as perceived by the vocational college leaders. However, Abdul Hamid and Norzaini (2010) found that the level of SA among the secondary students in a rural area in Malaysia varies from moderate to high. In contrast, Plucker (1996) found a low to moderate variation in SA among students in rural middle and high schools. Thus, it is observed that the perceived level of SA varies across schools.

In conclusion, the vocational college leaders possessed a highlevel of SL. They perceived the level of OB in schools as ranging from moderate to high. It is also found that the in-service trainingwas very efficient and beneficial to the vocational college leaders. Also, from their perspective, vocational college students exhibited a high level of SA as stated in the Malaysian Education Development Plan (2013 – 2025).

Strategic Leadership Practices (SL) in Relation to the Malaysian Technical and Vocational Education Students' Aspiration Outcomes (SA)

This subsection discusses the multi-dimensionality of SL and the direct relationship on SA. CFA was run to confirm the multi-dimensional constructs of SL. The study also evaluated the validity and reliability of the multi-dimensional constructs. In addition, the organizational capabilities constructs and the individual characteristics constructs were analyzed separately. Both models exhibited convergent validity and internal reliability.

Based on the results of the revised model of the organizational capabilities, it may be concluded that the vocational college leaders only possessed three out of five attributes suggested by Davies (2004) and Davies and Davies (2006; 2009) which are strategic orientation, strategic intervention and strategic alignment.The revised model of the individual characteristics reveals that the vocational college leaders possessed all four attributes suggested by Davies (2004) and Davies and Davies (2006; 2009) which are restlessness, absorptive capacity, adaptive capacity and wisdom. Further analysis was conducted to test the existence of the second order model of SL. The sampled data showed no proof of second order model of SL. A second-order factor model is indicated when first-order factors are explained by some higher-order factor structure (Schumacker et al., 1996). In such manner, SL is treated as a seven-factor model throughout the analysis (a combination of three attributes from organizational capabilities and four attributes from individual characteristics). This finding contradicts Hairuddin (2012), which deduces SL as a six-factor model. Other studies established SL as a nine-factor model (Adelakun, 2015; Ali, 2013; Nazifah, 2012). It is worth noting that the three research by Adelakun (2015), Ali (2013) and Nazifah (2012) use only descriptive analysis to describe the model. However, Hairuddin (2012) uses the same technique as this study but in the context of national primary school leaders.

This study further found that the vocational college leaders possessed seven strategic leadership practices as suggested by Davies (2004) and Davies and Davies (2006; 2009). These practices are strategic orientation, strategic alignment, strategic intervention, restlessness, absorptive capacity, adaptive capacity and wisdom.

However, the study did not find a direct causal effect between SL and SA. This finding is consistent with the findings of Bruggencate et al. (2012), Vidoni and Grassetti (2008), Ross and Gray (2006a), Ross and Gray (2006b), Witziers et al. (2003), Leithwood et al. (1999) and Hallinger and Heck

(1996). It is possible that the school leaders' leadership style is direct to the teachers but indirect to the students. Thus, the relationship between leadership and students' achievement was proven to have an indirect causal effect with the presence of another factor (i.e. mediator). Various research have identified several factors as determinants of leadership and students' achievement such as parental education (Vidoni & Grassetti, 2008), effective teaching and effective teacher learning (Robinson et al., 2008), teachers' commitment and teachers' efficacy (Ross & Gray, 2006a), teachers' belief about their capacity and their professional commitment (Ross and Gray, 2006b) and positive instructional climate in schools (Hallinger et al., 1996). Thus, it is evidentthat the relationship between leadership and students' achievement will have a significant effect on the presence of a mediator. This conclusion is in congruence with the findings of the study that empirically proved the significant indirect causal effect on the relationship between SL and SA with the presence of OB and IST as mediators. The two following sub-chapters further elaborate the findings.

Organizational Bureaucracy (OB) in Relation to the Malaysian Technical and Vocational Education Students' Aspiration Outcomes

To confirm the multi-dimensional constructs of OB, CFA was run, and the validity and reliability of the constructs were evaluated. As a result, a six-factor model that established the convergent validity and internal reliability was extracted with hierarchy of authority (HA), rules and regulations (RR), procedural specification (PS), technical competencies (TC), impersonality (IM) and division of labour (DL). Further analysis through the measurement model and the structural model of the TVESAI deduced only two underlying factors with regard to the TVESAI: RR (rules and regulations) and TC (technical competencies).

With regard to rules and regulations, in vocational colleges, official documentations of rules and regulations are in place. Adherence to rules ensures uniformity of procedures and operations and helps maintain organizational stability (Helriegel et al., 2001). Reliance on rules and regulations leads to treating employees impersonally and evaluations are done according to objective data. With respect to technical competencies, a system of promotion exists in vocational colleges, which are usually based on qualifications and achievement, meritocracy and seniority. Technical competencies constitute career enhancement.

The study found a substantial direct causal effect between OB and SA in the context of the Malaysian Technical and Vocational Education students' aspiration outcomes (magnitude of .63 standardized direct causal effect). Thus, the students' aspiration outcome, of which are leadership skills, national identity and ethics and spirituality, are directly influenced by the factors of OB (rules and regulations and technical competencies). The finding suggests that emphasis on OB increases the outcomes of the vocational students' aspiration.

The finding is in contrast with Chubb and Moe (1988, 1990) who argue organizational bureaucracy in public schools dampen educational effectiveness. Based on their research involving public and private schools' national survey data, they conclude that private schools outperformed public schools by having methods of institutional control and responsiveness to environments that were widely believed to produce educational effectiveness. Public schools acted as bureaucratic agents with multiple stakeholders but the decision-making process of the bureaucratic agent is tied to the bureaucratic process, thus, leaving the actual consumers (the students) of educational services at a disadvantage. Similarly, Bohte (2001) found a negative relationship between school bureaucracy and student performance. The research points out that as the level of bureaucracy increases (in terms of the percentage of central administrators, campus administrators and teachers), it is found to negatively affect students' passing rates on standardized reading, arithmetic, and writing test, as well as student performance on the Scholastic Assessment Test (SAT).

Nonetheless, Smith and Meier (1994) argue that bureaucracy's negative predictive power on students' performance was only marginal. In other words, the negative relationship between bureaucracy and school performance should be viewed based on causal logic. Their results suggest that bureaucracy mediates the trade-offs that schools face in responding to their task environments. Bureaucracy gives a strong impact on secondary goals such as attendance rates and graduation rates. Although bureaucracy is often judged by higher-order goals such as test scores, administrators have less control over those outputs. That is to say, bureaucracy does not dampen school performance, but it is the results of responding to lower performing schools (Smith & Meier, 1995; Meier, Polinard & Wrinkle, 2000). Thus, in the context of the Malaysian Technical and Vocational Education, organizational bureaucracy positively affects students' aspiration outcomes.

Furthermore, the study has also disclosed a significant indirect causal effect between SL and SA through OB (magnitude of .43 standardized indirect causal effect) which made OB the mediating factor between SL and SA. This result suggests that OB exhibits an indirect causal effect on leadership skills, national identity and ethics, and spirituality. The finding is in accordance with the finding by Wenglinsky (1997) that bureaucracy indirectly improved student achievement in mathematic scores across the United States in 1992 (Grades 4, 8 and 12) when spending on central administration at district levels was increased. The improvement must be due to the school administrators' help in improving the learning environments, and more administrators could contribute to advance educational improvement strategies.

Hence, SA will increase if joint attention is paid to both SL and SA. In other words, emphasis on the factors of OB (rules and regulations and technical competencies) would have increased the students' aspiration outcomes in relation to their leadership skills, national identity and ethics and spirituality. This research shows that OB positively and directly influenced SA. Taking the notion of Smith and Meier (1994), the presence of school bureaucracies in vocational colleges help to improve students' performance by placing the appropriate rules and regulations to enhance learning. OB also was observed to mediate the relationship between SL and SA possibly through the element of technical competencies. With OB putting everything in place, the Malaysian vocational college leaders could effectively strive for better school performance.

In-Service Training Effectiveness (IST) in Relation to the Malaysian Technical and Vocational Education Students' Aspiration Outcomes

This subsection discusses the multi-dimensionality of IST and the direct and indirect relationships with SA. Based on CFA which was run to confirm the multi-dimensional constructs of IST and the validity and reliability tests It will also discussa five-factor model as suggested by Guskey (2000) which established the convergent validity and internal reliability which was extracted with *Reaction* (participant's reaction), *Support* (organizational support and change), *Learning* (participant's learning), *New* (new skills and knowledge), and (students' learning outcomes).

The study found a direct causal effect between IST and SA in the context of the Malaysian Technical and Vocational Education students' aspiration outcomes (magnitude of .21 standardized direct causal effect). Thus, the students' aspiration outcomes which are leadership skills, national identity and ethics and spirituality are directly influenced by the five factors of IST.

The finding suggested that emphasis on IST increases the outcomes of the vocational students' aspiration.

The finding is aligned with the arguments of Che Mohd Zulkifli (2014), Thompson (2003) and Shanti (1998); in which in-service training develops new knowledge and skills among school staffs. Cohen and Hill (2001) found that in-service training related to curriculum helped the teachers in teaching and influenced students' achievements. In another study, Garet (2001) studied mathematics teachers' involvement in the in-service training programmes and concluded that the teachers are pedagogically prepared to implement change in teaching practice, improve in knowledge and teaching skills.

As empirically proven in this research, in-service training was also found to influence students' performance in many past studies(e.g. Hanushek, 1986; Andrew, 2002; Borich, 2003; Clotfelter et al., 2007; Guskey, 1995, 2000; Hawley & Valli, 1999; Joyce & Showers, 2002; Fullan, Hill, & Crevola, 2006).McCutchen et al. (2002) in his study of phonetics found that students' achievement under teachers who attended phonetics training outperformed the students who were taught by untrained teachers. Angrist and Lavy (2001) discovered that the in-service training received by school teachers has resulted in improved examination results. Jacob and Lefgren (2004), however, found marginal increases in in-service training have no statistically significant effect on students' performance.

The study has also found a significant indirect causal effect between SL and SA through IST (magnitude of .11 standardized indirect causal effect) which made IST as the mediating factor between SL and SA. This result suggests that IST exhibits an indirect causal effect on leadership skills, national identity and ethics and spirituality. The result complements Cheng and Tsui's (1996) results that suggest in-service training that supports teachers' performance, expertise development and teachers' education has an indirect relationship with students' achievements. Hence, SA will increase if the emphasis is given to both SL and SA. In other words, the emphasis on IST would have increased the students' aspiration outcomes in relation to the leadership skills, national identity and ethics and spirituality.

Based on these findings, it may be said that IST is an important component that contributes to SA. IST directly influences SA and indirectly mediates the leadership roles of the vocational school leaders and the aspirations of the vocational college students. Thus, IST elements are substantial in educational planning.

The Malaysian Technical and Vocational Education Students' Aspiration Outcomes (SA)

This subsection discusses the underlying factors of SA. The CFA and validity and reliability tests resulted in a six-factor model that established the construct validity, convergent validity and internal reliability extracted with BP (bilingual proficiency), *Know* (knowledge), *Leader* (leadership skills), ID (national identity), *Think* (thinking skills) and *Ethics* (ethics and spirituality). Further analysis through the measurement model and the structural model of the TVESAI deduced only three underlying factors with regard to the TVESAI. The three factors are *Leader* (leadership skills), ID (national identity) and *Ethics* (ethics and spirituality).

In the Malaysian Education Development Plan (2013-2025), leadership skills comprise four elements: entrepreneurship, resilience, emotional intelligence and strong communication skills. According to Amirianzadeh et al. (2010), Thompson (2012) and Fincher et al. (2007), one way to acquire leadership skills is through co-curricular activities in school. Through co-curricular activities, the four elements of leadership skills could be developed. This is parallel to the findings by numerous scholars who state that co-curricular activities enhance the elements of leadership skills such as self-resilience (Abd. Razzaq et al., 2010), strong communication skills (Sitra & Sasidhar, 2005; Wictor & Andersson, 2012) and emotional intelligence (Robinson, 2009; Hsu, 2011; Thompson, 2012; Guimba et al., 2011; Fincher & Shalka, 2009).

With regard to national identity, the Malaysian Education Development Plan (2013-2025) states that all students should identify themselves proudly as Malaysians regardless of their backgrounds. The government sees that the effort in establishing national identity is vital and can be done through the education system (Ahmad Fawzi, 1987). As a multi-racial country, the process of national integration among various ethnicities will always be a challenge to Malaysia (Rabaskha & Shepsle, 1972). For instance, Santhiram (1999) and Hazri (2007) found that ethnicity influences students' interaction and unity in schools.

The third underlying factor of SA within the TVESAI model, ethics and spirituality' is contextually inclusive of three attributes stated inthe Malaysian Education Development Plan (2013-2025): spirituality, integrity, and civic responsibility. From the Islamic perspective, ethics and spirituality are intertwined (Darraz, 1973; Al-Attas, 1978; Syed Ali Ashraf, 1990). One could not be ethical and at the same time has a low level of spirituality or vice versa (Syed Ali Ashraf, 1990). Thus, Islamic education and moral education in schools are designed to fulfil the aspiration outcomes. The goal of Islamic and moral education is to establish and develop aspects of human perfection that include physical, spiritual, mental and social development so that children can devote themselves to God and to do good to others. Thus, emphasis on building students' ethics and spirituality will develop the ability to faceadult life with sound judgments.

IMPLICATIONS OF THE STUDY

The findings of the study give rise to several implications, theoretically and empirically. The theoretical implications are related to the contributions made to the body of knowledge (theory) pertaining to factors contributing to SA in the context of the vocational colleges. The practical implications, in contrast, contribute to practices of school leaders and students in the vocational college environment. Each implication is discussed separately.

Theoretical Implications

The theoretical implications of this research underpin the causal effects (direct and indirect) among TVESAI variables. Some of the theoretical implications are as follows:

1. There was evidence of construct validity and reliability pertaining to the four scales (Kline, 2010; Hair et al., 2010; Byrne, 2010); SL, OB, IST and SA established through the application of rigorous statistical analyses on the instruments under study.

2. A seven-factor model compared to the nine-factor model in the United Kingdom (Davies & Davies, 2004; 2006; 2009) explains SL in the context of the Malaysian vocational college leaders. These factors are strategic orientation, strategic intervention, strategic alignment, restlessness, adaptive capacity, adaptive capacity and wisdom. Quantitative evaluation and replication need to be carried out with particular reference to the SL across all school types in Malaysia to confirm the seven-factor model of SL.

3. The findings from the West state that bureaucracy has little impact (Meier et al., 2000; Smith & Lariner, 2004) or has an adverse influence

on students' performance (Bohte, 2001). However, capturing the effect of the Eastern school environment, OB is explained by a two-factor model in the context of the Malaysian vocational colleges. The analysis unveils a positive impact of OB (rules and regulations, technical competence) on SA in relation to the OB literature.

4. The five-factor model of IST confirms the importance of continuous professional development (CPD) for school leaders. Thus, it is added to the IST literature that CPD improves school leaders' knowledge and skills, increases organization support and changes and affects students' learning outcomes (Che Mohd Zulkifli, 2014; Clotfelter et al., 2007; Fullan, Hill & Crevola, 2006; Borich, 2003; Andrew, 2002; Joyce & Showers, 2002; McCutchen, 2002; Cohen & Hill, 2001; Garet, 2001; Angrist & Lavy, 2000; Hawley & Valli, 1999; Shanti, 1998; Guskey, 1995, 2000; Hanushek, 1986).

5. The research found that a three-factor model in the context of Malaysian vocational students explains SA. As far as the researcher's knowledge is concerned, this is the first research carried out to quantify SA from the Malaysian Education Development Plan (2013-2025) paradigm. The interpretation of the results shows that the vocational college students only possess three out of six students' aspiration outcomes in relation to the SA literature. The three factors are ethics and spirituality (Norazani et al., 2004; Syed Ali Ashraf, 1990; Al-Attas, 1978; Darraz, 1973), national identity (Hazri, 2007; Santhiram, 1999; Ahmad Fawzi, 1987; Rabaskha & Shepsle, 1972) and leadership skills (Wictor & Andersson, 2012; Thompson, 2012; Guimba et al., 2011; Hsu, 2011; Amirianzadeh et al., 2010; Abd. Razzaq, 2010; Robinson, 2009; Fincher & Shalka, 2009; Sitra & Sasidhar, 2005).

6. The study theoretically establishes the existence of the mediation effects of OB (Wenglinsky, 1997) and IST (Cheng &Tsui, 1996) on the relationship between SL and SA with particular reference to the Malaysian vocational colleges. Both OB and IST fully mediate the relationship between SL and SA. The mediation effect is one of the research gaps concerning the researched variables under study as far as the researcher's knowledge is concerned. In both the Western and Eastern settings, the mediation effects are not explored.

7. TVESAI is the first suggested model in the Eastern cultural setting and most probably in the Western setting too. Little information is available regarding the relationship between the four variables

as one model. Limited literature reviews are found discussing the link between any of the two variables in the study. Most researchers discuss each variable separately.

Practical Implications

In addition to the theoretical implications above, the study provides demonstrable practical contributions to the applied research in the context of the Malaysian vocational college environment. Such practical contributions underpin the initiatives concerning the vocational college leaders and the vocational college students. The practical implications that contribute to the school leaders' practices and students' performance in the vocational college environment are listed below:

1. In the pursuit of the excellent performance of the vocational college leaders, the findings of this study would help educational administrators to introduce programmes and courses that inculcate strategic leadership practices among vocational college leaders.

2. The findings provide insights to policy-makers, in particular, the human resource managers. The results of the research can be used to justify the direction of designing, developing and implementing appropriate learning and performance improvement interventions, so that SL, OB, IST, and SA could be continuously enhanced among the vocational college leaders. It could lead to fully equipped and knowledgeable vocational college leaders, which in turn might increase the organizational performance and boost the vocational students' performances.

3. The instruments developed and adopted for the TVESAI provides a valid tool for testing factors that influence the vocational students' aspiration outcomes. The Ministry of Education Malaysia can utilize the instruments as the guidelines for assessing the strategic leadership practices of school leaders, the level of organizational bureaucracy in schools, the effectiveness of the in-service training and the national students' aspiration outcomes.

4. With further modification and replication, the TVESAI provides a valid tool to study the strategic leadership practices of school leaders, the level of organizational bureaucracy in schools, the effectiveness of the in-service training and the national students' aspiration outcomes.

RECOMMENDATIONS OF THE STUDY

In the light of the conclusions derived, and the implications of the study, several recommendations may be made. The recommendations are divided into two parts: recommendations for the Division of Technical and Vocational Education, Ministry of Education Malaysia and recommendations for future research.

Recommendations for the Division of Technical and Vocational Education

To begin with, the study found that the vocational college leaders only possessed seven out of nine strategic leadership practices as suggested by Davies & Davies (2004, 2009), and strategic leadership does not directly affect students' aspiration outcomes. Thus, it is recommended that vocational college leaders possess all nine strategic leadership practices proposed by Davies and Davies (2004, 2009). Nonetheless, the strategic translation capability and strategic competencies capability were absent. Emphasis should be given to both organizational capabilities during in-service training for the vocational college leaders. A thorough study should be conducted on the effects of strategic leadership on students' aspiration because there was no relationship between the two variables. The question is whether there is certainly no effectof strategic leadership on students' aspiration, or we have been doing it (giving leadership training to the school leaders) wrongly.

Secondly, the study also reveals that only two elements of organizational bureaucracy, rules and regulation and technical competencies exist in the vocational college environment. In addition, organizational bureaucracy directly and significantly affects students' aspiration outcomes and mediates the relationship between strategic leadership practices and students' aspiration outcomes. Both of the elements, rules and regulations and technical competencies positively impact students' aspiration outcomes and strategic leadership practices. Thus, a system of rules and regulations should be periodically reviewed, updated and implemented, coupled with an appealing career advancement package based on technical competence. In terms of promotion, additional merits should be given to the vocational colleges' leaders for being school leaders.

Thirdly, the study indicates that in-service training benefits the vocational college leaders regarding the students' learning outcomes, contributions to the organization and development of teachers' new knowledge and skills. Further, in-service training directly and significantly affects students' aspiration outcomes, and mediates the relationship between strategic leadership practices and students' aspiration outcomes. It is irrefutable that the in-service training conducted by the Ministry is effective. To extend the effort, each vocational college leader should have a unique training plan based on his/her need. An individual-based training needs analysis (TNA) must be established before the vocational college leaders attend any course. Specifically, emphasis should be given to inculcate strategic leadership practices, understand how organizational bureaucracy could have a positive impact on the organization and students' learning outcomes and educate vocational college students to ensure they possess all six student aspiration outcomes as suggested by the Malaysian Education Development Plan (2013-2025).

Fourthly, the vocational college students only possess three out of six student aspiration outcomes as suggested by the Malaysian Education Development Plan (2013-2025). Half of the objectives of the Malaysian Education Development Plan (2013-2025) are to groom the Malaysian students to possess six (6) student aspiration outcomes. Compared to other types of schools, vocational colleges concentrate 70% of the learning time teaching vocational subjects. Thus, it can be one of the reasons why the elements of knowledge (which focus on basic knowledge of mathematics, science, geography and history), bilingual proficiency and thinking skills did not emerge in the TVESAI. Accordingly, priority should be given to the three missing attributes of student aspiration outcomes. One of the possibilities is to re-examine the contact hours allocated to the academic and vocational subjects. The elements of bilingual proficiency and thinking skills should be applied in the vocational subjects wherever appropriate.

Recommendations for Future Research

The findings from the study highlight a number of new avenues that could be explored in future studies. To begin with, the multi-dimensional constructs of the strategic leadership practices need to be explored further across all school types (e.g. national schools, national-type schools and religious schools) in Malaysia to develop a strategic leadership practices inventory for the Malaysian school leaders.The multi-dimensional constructs of students' aspiration outcomes should also be further explored in all school types (e.g. national schools, national-type schools and religious schools) in Malaysia to develop a students' aspiration outcomes inventory for Malaysian students.In addition, the structure of the TVESAI should be re-examined and replicated in the different cultural groups. In the re-examination process, the headmasters, the principals, the assistant principals and other levels of school administrative leaders should be treated as separate group samples. A multi-group analysis using SEM can be carried out on the same dataset to observe the structural differences in the TVESAI model.

Further investigations concerning organizational bureaucracy and in-service training effectiveness may also be worthwhile. These variables should be further tested as moderators. This type of examination provides the extent of the effects of organizational bureaucracy and in-service training effectiveness towards students' aspiration outcomes. On top of that, the predictors of SL, OB, and IST may have an influence on other behavioural aspects of the students' performance in the context of the Malaysian school system. The psychometric indices of TVESAI should be tested further in future studies to have a broader scope overall and understanding in different settings of the Eastern countries. Last, but not least, the findings of this study indicate no relationship between strategic leadership practices on students' aspiration. Based on this, further study on the linkage between the two variables to identify factors that hinder the development of this dimension and suggest a possible solution to the problem would be desirable.

CONCLUSION

There have been many empirical studies on the predictors of SA in the Western school setting. None of the studies cover the variables under study: SL, OB and IST on SA in one research. Most research separately tests the effects SL, OB, and IST on SA, especially in the context of the Eastern school setting, specifically in the vocational colleges. Quantitatively, through the application of CFA and SEM, this study successfully deduces the underlying factors of SL, OB, IST and SA by instrument validation. Findings were discussed in relation to the Malaysian vocational colleges setting.

SA was found as a three-factor model, which consists of leadership skills, national identity, and ethics and spirituality. Interestingly, there is a strong direct causal effect of OB on SA with a two-factor model (rules and regulations and technical competencies). The direct causal effect suggests that OB directly predicts SA. Thus, more emphasis needs to be given to the organizational bureaucracy to increase the students' aspiration outcomes. The study also found a direct causal effect of IST, a five-factor model (participant's reaction), organizational support and change, participant's learning, new skills and knowledge and students' learning outcomes on SA. Nevertheless, the study found no significant relationship between SL and SA. Despite the unsupported hypothesis, the finding is consistent with other research findings that found near zero relationships between SL and SA. With the presence of a mediator, the relationship between SL and SA is significant. In addition, OB and IST fully mediate the relationship between SL and SA, which is a significant theoretical contribution to the body of knowledge.

In conclusion, this study deduces significant relationships between OB Þ SA and IST Þ SA and also, both OB and IST mediate the relationship between SL and SA. Based on these findings, it is vital for the Ministry of Education, Malaysia to pay attention to the strategic leadership practices of school leaders, elements of organizational bureaucracy and in-service training programmes to directly impact the vocational students' aspiration outcomes as visioned by the Malaysian Education Development Plan (2013-2025).

REFERENCES

Al- Quran Nul Kareem

Abd. Razzaq, A. R., Md. Yunos, J., Hashim, J. & Sawah, N. (2010). Penerapan dan Penguasaan Kemahiran Generik dalam Proses P&P bagi Program Pengurusan Hotel dan Katering di Politeknik ke Arah Keperluan Industri. *Kemahiran Insaniah: Kajian di Institusi-Institusi Pengajian.*inEsa, A. & Mustafa, M. Z (pp. 153-182). BatuPahat: UnversitiTunHussien Onn.

Abdul Hamid, A.R. &Norzaini, A. (2010). Educational Aspiration among First-Generation Students and their Parental Influence towards Pursuing Tertiary Education.*Procedia Social and Behavioral Sciences*, 7, 414–418.

Abdul-Wahhab, M. (1997). *MokhtasarSirat Al-RasoulSallahAllahuAlaihiwaSallam, [Summary of the Sirah of the Messenger Peace Be Upon Him]*. Damascus: Dar Al-Fayha.

Adair, J. (2002) *Effective strategic* leadership. London: Macmillan.

Adelakun, S.F. (2015). *Strategic leadership and self-efficacy practices among school leaders of International Schools in Kuala Lumpur* (Unpublished master dissertation).Malaysia: IIUM.

Ahmad Fawzi, B. (1987). *Isu-IsuPerpaduanNasional: Cabaran, Pencapaiandan Masa Depan.* Kuala Lumpur: UUM.

Al-Attas, Syed Muhammad al-Naquib. (1978). *Islam and Secularism*. Kuala Lumpur: Muslim Youth Movement of Malaysia.

Al-Baihaqi, A. B. A. (n.d.). *Al-Sunan Al-Kubra*. Beirut: Dar Al-Fikr.

Al-Mawardi, A. A. M. (1983). *Al-Ahkam Al-Sultaniyah, [The Sultanic Rules]*. Beirut: Dar Al-Kutob Al-Ilmiyah.

Al-Wakil, M. S. (1988). *Al-Qiyadahwa Al-Jondiyyah fi Al-Islam [Leadership and Military in Islam]*. Egypt: Al-Wafa" Littiba"awa Al-Nashr.

Ali, A. (2013). *The relationship between strategic leadership practices and self-efficacy among school leaders in Republic of Maldives* (Unpublished master dissertation).Malaysia: IIUM.

Ali, A. Y. (1985). *The Holy Qur'an, English Translation of the Meanings and Commentary*. Al-Madinah al-Munawwarah: King Fahd Complex for the Printing of the Holy Qur"an.

Aliaga, M. and Gunderson, B. (2002). *Interactive Statistics*. Thousand Oaks: Sage.

Amirianzadeh, P. J., Jaafari, P., Ghourchian, N. & Jowkar, B. (2010). College Student Leadership Competencies Development:A Model. *International Journal for Cross-Disciplinary Subjects in Education (IJCDSE), 1*(3), 168-172. Retrieved from http://infonomics-societv.org.

Anastasi, A. & Urbina, S. (1997). *Psychological testing (7thed.)*. Upper Saddle River. NJ: Prentice-Hall.

Anderson, B. D. (1970). *Bureaucratization and alienation: An empirical study in secondary schools* (Doctoral dissertation). Canada: University of Toronto.

Anderson, S., &Wanberg, K. (1991). A congruent validity model of emergent leadership in groups. <u>Small Group Research, 22</u>(3).

Andrew, R (2002). *Reflective Teaching: Effective and Research-Based Professional Practice*. London: Continuum International Group Leader.

Andrews, F. M. (1984). Construct validity and error components of survey measures: A structural modeling approach. *Public OpinionQuarterly*, 48, 409—422.

Angrist, J. D. and Lavy, V. (2001), 'Does teacher training affect pupil learning? Evidence from matched comparisons in Jerusalem public schools', *Journal of Labor Economics*, *19*(2), 343-369.

Ary, D.; Jacobs, L. C. &Razavich, A. (2002). *Introduction to research in education (6thed.)* (241—274). Wadsworth Thomson Leaving.

Astone, N. M. &McLanahan, S. S. (1991). Family structure, parental practices and high school completion. *American Sociological Review*, *56*(3), 309-320.

Azam, O. &Zainurrin, D. (2011). Professional Development among Academic Staff at Selected Malaysian Public Universities: Preliminary Findings of the Impact of the Basic Teaching Methodology Course (BTMC). *International Journal of Business and Social Science. 2*(11); 125-134.

Baker, T.L. (1994), *Doing Social Research (2nd Edn.).* New York: McGraw-Hill Inc.

Barreiro, P.L. &Albandoz, J.P. (2001). *Population and Sample.* Retrieved from http://optimierung.mathematik.unikl.de/mamaeusch/veroeffentlichungen/ver_texte/sampling_en.pdf

Barth, R. (1990). *Improving Schools From Within: Teachers, Parents and Principals Can Make the Difference.* San Francisco: Jossey-Bass.

Basbous, A. M. (1988). *Fan Al-Qiyadah fi Al-Islam, [The Art of Leadership in Islam].* Jordan: Maktabat Al-Manar.

Bass, B., &Avolio, B. (1985). *The multifactor leadership questionnaire.* Palo Alto: Consulting Psychologists Press.

Bayton, J. A. (1943). Interrelations between Levels of Aspiration, Performance, and Estimates of Past Performance. *Journal of Experimental Psychology, 33*(1), 1-21.

Beare, H. (2001) *Creating the future* school. London, Routledge Falmer.

Beekun, R. I. &Badawi, J. (1999). *Leadership: An Islamic Perspective.* Maryland: Amana Publishers.

Bennett, J., Braund, M., &Lubben, F. (2010). *The Impact of Targeted Continuing Professional Development (CPD) On Teachers' Professional Practice in Science. Main Report.*Report commissioned by the DFCS through the National Science Learning Centre. York: University of York, Department of Educational Studies.

Bennet, A. & Bennet, D. (2008). Moving from knowledge to wisdom, from ordinary consciousness to extraordinary consciousness. *The Journal of Information and Knowledge Management Systems, 38*(1), 7-15. Retrieved from: http://jemi.edu.pl/all-issues/vol10/issue1/article1/full

Bennis, W. &Nanus, B. (1985). *Leaders; The Strategies for Taking Charge.* New York: Harper and Row.

Bierly, P. E., Kessler, E. H. and Christensen, E. W. (2000). Organizational learning, knowledge and wisdom. *Journal of Organizational Change Management, 13*(6), 595-618.

Black, J. A. &Bola, K. B. (1996) Assessing the organizational capacity to change, in: A. Heene& R. Sanchez (Eds) *Competence-based strategic measurement* (Chichester, John Wiley & Sons).

Blanchard, K. and Peale, N. (1988). *The Power of Ethical Management.* New York: Fawcett Crest.

Blunch, N. J. (2008). *Introduction to Structural Equation Modelling Using SPSS and AMOS.* California: SAGE Publications.

Bola, K. B., &Hooijberg, R. (2000). Strategic leadership research: Moving on. *Leadership Quarterly, 11*, 515-549.

Bohte, J. (2001). School bureaucracy and student performance at the local level. *Public Administration Review, 61*(1), 92-99. doi: 10.1111/0033-3352.00008.

Boisot, M. (1995). Preparing for turbulence, in: B. Garratt (Ed.). *Developing strategic thought* (London, McGraw-Hill).

Bollen, K. A., & Long, J. S. (1993). *Testing structural equation models.* Newbury Park, CA: Sage.

Bolt, J. F. (1996). Developing three-dimensional leaders. In *Leader of the future, ed. Frances Hesselbein, Marshall Goldsmith, and Richard Beckhard*, 161-174. San Francisco: Jossey-Bass Publishers.

Borich, G. D (2003). *Effective Teaching Methods (5ᵗʰ Ed).* New Jersey: Prentice-Hall.

Bourque, L., & Clark, V. (1992). *Processing Data: The Survey Example (Sage University Paper series on Quantitative Applications in the Social Sciences.* Newbury Park, CA: Sage

Bowling, A. (2009). *Research methods in health: Investigative Health and Health Services* (3rded.). New York: McGraw-Hill.

Brislin, R., Loner, W. and Thorndike, R. (1973). *Cross-cultural Research Methods.* New York, NY: Wiley & Sons.

Brookover, W. (1979). *School Social Systems and Student Achievements: Schools Can Make a Difference.* New York: Praeger.

Bruggencate, G. T, Luyten, H., Scheerens, J. &Sleegers, P. (2012).Modelling the Influence of School Leaders on Student Achievement: How Can School Leaders Make a Difference?*Educational Administration Quarterly, 84*(4), 699-732.

Bryson, J. M. (2003), *Strategic Planning for Public and Non-profit Organization.* San Francisco, CA: Jossey-Bass.

Buchmann, C., & Dalton, B. (2002). Interpersonal influence and educational aspirations in 12 countries; The importance of Institutional Context. *Sociology of Education, 74*(2), 99- 122.

Burgleman R. A, & Grove, A. S. (1996) Strategic dissonance. *California Management Review, 38*(2), 8–28.

Burns, J. M. (1978). *Leadership.* New York: Harper and Row.

Bush, T. (2003) *Theories of Educational Management,* 3rd edn, London: Sage.

Byrne, B. M. (2010). *Structural equation modeling with AMOS,* (2nd ed.). New York: Routledge.

Byrum, T. B. (2008). *Teachers' perceptions of the effect of principal leadership on teacher retention.* Retrieved from http://search.proquest.com/docview/304367113?accountid=12964.

Campbell, D. T. & Fiske, D. W. (1959). Convergent and discriminant validation by the multi-traits multi-method matrix. *PsychologicalBulletin, 56,* 81-105.

Canella Jr., A. A., & Monroe, M. J. (1997). Contrasting perspectives on strategic leaders: Toward a more realistic view of top managers. *Journal of Management, 23,* 213–237.

Centre for Public Policy Studies, Asian Strategy and Leadership Institute (ASLI-CPPS), Association for the Promotion of Human Rights (PROHAM), Institute of Ethnic Studies, UniversitiKebangsaan Malaysia (KITA-UKM). (2012). *Report on Education Reform and Process of Consultation.* Malaysia. Retrieved from http://www.cpps.org.my/upload/EDUCATION_REFORM_IN_MALAYSIA_REPORT_2012.pdf

CheMohdZulkifli, C. O. (2014). The Need for In-Service Training for Teachers and It's Effectiveness In School.*International Journal for Innovation Education and Research. 2*(11), 1-9.

Cheng, Y. C. (2000). Educational Reforms in the New Century: Multiple Intelligence and Globalization, Localization and Individualization. In the Chinese Educational Research Association (ed.), *New Vision of Educational Development in the New Century* (pp. 1-41).

Cheng, Y.C. &Tsui, K. T. (1996). Total Teacher Effectiveness: New Conception and Improvement. *International Journal of Educational Management.6,* 7-17. doi: http://dx.doi.org/10.1108/09513549610151659.

Cheung, G. W., &Rensvold, R. B. (2000). Assessing extreme and acquiescence response sets in cross-cultural research using structural equation modeling. *Journal of Cross-Cultural Psychology,31,* 187–212.

Child, J. (1972). Organizational structure, environment, and performance: The role of strategic choice. *Sociology, 6,* 1–22.

Chuan, C. L. (2006). Sample size estimation using Krejcie and Morgan and Cohen statistical power analysis: A comparison. *JurnalPenyelidikan IPBL, 7,* 78-86.

Chubb, J., & Moe, T. (1988). Politics, markets and the organization of schools. *American Political Science Review, 82*(4), 1065-1087. doi: 10.2307/1961750.

Chubb, J., & Moe, T. (1990). *Politics, markets and America's schools.* Washington, D.C.: The Brookings Institution Press.

Clotfelter, C. T., Helen F. L. and Jacob L. V. (2007). *Teacher Credentials and Student Achievement in High School: A Cross-Subject Analysis with Student Fixed Effects.* Working Paper #11. Washington, DC: CALDER. doi: 10.3386/w13617.

Cohen, W. M. &Levinthal, D. A. (1990) Absorptive capacity: a new perspective on learning and innovation, *Administrative Science Quarterly*, *35*, 128–152

Cohen, D. K. and Hill, H. C. (2001). *Learning Policy: When State Education Reform Works*. New Haven: Yale University Press.

Cohen, L.; Manion, L. & Morrison, K. (2008). *Research methods in education* (6th ed.). London & New York: Routledge Taylor & Francis Group. 133—164.

Cochran, W.G. (1977). *Sampling Techniques*. 3rd Edition. Wiley: New York.

Coltman, T., Devinney, T. M., Midgley, D. F., &Venaik, S. (2008). *Formative versus reflective measurement models: Two applications of formative measurement*. Retrieved from http://works.bepress.com/tcoltman/6.

Covey, S. R. (1996). Three roles of the leader in the new paradigm, in Hesselbein, F., Goldsmith, M. and Beckhard, R.), *The Leader of the Future: New Visions, Strategies, and Practices for the Next Era*, Jossey-Bass, San Francisco, CA, 149-59.

Craft, A. (2000). *Continuing Professional Development: A practical guide for teachers and schools*. London: Routledge Falmer.

Creswell, J. W. (2003). *Research design: Qualitative, quantitative and mixed method approaches* (2nd ed). United States of America: Sage Publications, Inc.

Creswell, J. W. (2005). *Educational research: Planning, conducting and evaluating quantitative and qualitative research* (2nd ed.), Upper Saddle River, N.J.: Pearson Merrill Prentice Hall.

Creswell, J. W. (2009). *Research Design: Qualitative, Quantitative, and Mixed Methods Approaches*. 3rd Edition. Los Angeles: Sage Publications.

Cronbach, L. J. (1989). Construct validity after thirty years. In R. Linn (ed.) *Intelligence measurement, theory and public policy*. Urbana: University of Illinois Press.

Crossan, M., Dusya, V. &Nanjad, L. (2008). Transcendant Leadership: Strategic Leadership in Dynamic Environments. *The Leadership Quarterly, 19*, 569-581.

Cuban, L. (1988). *The Managerial Imperative and the Practice of Leadership in Schools.* Albany, NY: State University of New York Press.

Darraz, Muhammad Abdullah. (1973). *Dustur al-Akhlaq fi al-Qur'an.* Beirut: Muassasah al-Risalah.

Davies, B. (2003) Rethinking strategy and strategic leadership in schools, *Education Management & Administration, 31*, 295–312

Davies, B. and Davies, B. J. (2004). Strategic Leadership. *School Leadership and Management, 24* (1), 29-38.

Davies, B.(2006). *Leading the Strategically Focused School: Success and Sustainability.* CA: Sage Publications,Thousand Oaks.

Davies, B. and Davies, B. J. (2009). Strategic leadership, in Davies, B. (Ed.), *The Essentials of School Leadership*, 2nd ed., Sage Publications, Thousand Oaks, CA, pp. 13-35.

Davies, B. & Ellison, L. (2003). *The New Strategic Direction and Development of the School: Key Frameworks for School Improvement Planning.* New York: Routledge Falmer.

Day, C. (1999). Professional development and reflective practice: purposes, processes and partnerships. *Pedagogy, Culture and Society, 7*(2), 221–233.

Delva, M. D., Kirby, J. R., Knapper, C. K. & Birtwhistle, R.V. (2002). Postal survey of approaches to learning among Ontario Physicians: Implications for continuing medical education. *Britsh Medical Journal, 325*, 1218-1222.

Dembo, T. (1976). The dynamics of anger. In J. De Rivera (Ed.), *Field theory as human-science* (324-422). New York: Gardner Press.

Dienesch, R., &Liden, R. (1986). Leader-exchange exchange model of leadership: A critique and further development. *Academy of Management Journal, 11*, 618-634.

Donmoyer, R. (2011). Cultural connections in leadership education and practice. *The International Journal of Leadership in Education, 14*(1), 119-125.

Eacott, S. (2008). Strategy in educational leadership: in search of unity. *Journal of Educational Administration, 46*(3), 353-75. DOI: http://dx.doi.org/10.1108/09578230810869284.

Edmonds, R. (1979). Some Schools Work and More Can. *Social Policy, March-April*, 28-32.

Edmunds, A. (1998). Content, concurrent and construct validity of the leadership skills inventory. *Roeper Review, 20*(4), 281-285.

Elmore, R. F. (2002). Unwarranted Intrusion. *Education Next, 2*(1), 30–35.

Etzioni, A. (1961). *A comparative analysis of complex organizations.* New York: Free Press.

Evers, C.W. (2010). Educational leadership: Philosophical issues, in Baker E; McGaw B; Peterson P (ed.), *International encyclopedia of education*, edn. 3rd, Amsterdam: Elsevier, 710 – 716.

Feldman, S. D. (1974). *Escape From the Doll's House: Women in Graduate and Professional School Education.* New York: McGraw-Hill.

Ferguson, G.A. (1981). *Statistical Analysis in PhD Education*, 5th ed., New York: McGraw Hill.

Fincher, J. &Shalka, T. R. (2009). Co-curricular Leadership Education: Considering Critical Questions. *Journal of Leadership Education, 8(1)*, 228-237. Retrieved from http://www.leadershipeducators.org.

Finkelstein, S., & Hambrick, D. C. (1996). *Strategic leadership: Top executives and their effects*. Minneapolis/St. Paul: West Publishing.

Fraenkel, J. R. & Norman, E. W. (2008). *How to design and evaluate research in education*. 7th ed. New York: McGraw-Hill.

Flouri, E. (2006). Non-resident fathers' relationships with their secondary school age children: Determinants and children's mental health outcomes. *Journal of Adolescence, 29*, 525–538.

Fullan, M., Hill, P., & Crevola, C. (2006). *Breakthrough*. Corwin Press.

Gardiner, J. W. (1940). The relation of certain personality variables to level of aspiration. *Journal of Psychology, 9*, 191-206.

Garet, M. S. (2001). What Makes Professional Development Effective? Results from a National Sample of Teachers. *American Education Research Journal. 38* (4), 915-945.

Gioia, D. A. & Thomas, J. G. (1996). Identity, image, and issue interpretation: sense making during strategic change in academia. *Administrative Science Quarterly, 41*, 370–403.

Goodall, J., Day, C., Lindsay, G., Muijs, D. and Harris, A. (2005). Evaluating the Impact of Continuing Professional Development. *Research Report*, 659, Department for Education and Skills.

Goodwin, R. (2002). On the edge of chaos: A delphi study of the changing role of the secondary principal (Doctoral Dissertation).

Gorard, S. (2005). Current contexts for research in educational leadership and management. *Educational Management Administration and Leadership, 33*(2), 155-164.

Graen, G., Novak, M., & Sommerkamp, P. (1982). The effects of leader-member exchange and job design on productivity and job satisfaction: Testing a dual attachment model. *Organizational Behavior and Human Performance, 30*, 109-131.

Gratton, L. (2000) *Living strategy: putting people at the heart of corporate purpose.* London: Financial Times–Prentice Hall.

Gray, J. (2000). *Causing Concern but Improving: A Review of Schools' Experience.* London: DfEE.

Greenleaf, R. (1977). *Servant Leadership; A Journey into the Nature of Legitimate Power and Greatness,* New York: Paulist Press.

Groundwater-Smith, S. (2000). *Evidence Based Practice – Towards Whole School Improvement.* Paper Presented to the Annual Conference Australian Association for Research in Education Sydney, 4-7 December 2000.

Guimba, W., Hashim, C. N., Hussien, S., Razikin, M. & Esteban, I. (2011). Leadership Experiences of Undergraduate Muslim Student Leaders: An Exploratory Case Study. *European Journal of Social Sciences, 20(1),* pg. 112-122. Retrieved from http://www.eurojournals.comtEJSS.

Guskey, T.R. (2000a) *Evaluating Professional Development,* Thousand Oaks, Ca.: Corwin Press.

Guskey, T. (2000b). Does it make a difference? Evaluating professional development. *Educational Leadership, 59* (6), 45-51.

Guskey, T. (1995). Professional Development in Education: In Search of the Optimal Mix.*In Professional Development in Education: New Paradigms and Practices.* (Guskey, T. & Huberman, M. Eds.) New York:Teachers College Press. 114-132.

Guskey, T. R. (1994). Professional development in education. In search of the optimal mix. Annual Meeting of the American Educational Research Association, New Orleans.

Guskey, T. R., & Sparks, D. (1991). What to consider when evaluating staff development. *Educational Leadership, 49*(3), 73-76.

Gutman, L. M. &Akerman, R. (2008). *Determinants of Aspirations.* Department for children, schools, and families (DCSF).

Hackman, M. and Johnson, C. (1991). *Leadership*. Prospects Heights: Waveland Press.

Hair, J. F., Black, W. C., Babin, B. J., & Anderson, R. E. (2010). *Multivariate data analysis* (7 ed.). Uppersaddle River, New Jersey: Pearson Education International.

Hairuddin, M. A. (2012). The quest for strategic Malaysian Quality National Primary School Leaders. *International Journal of Educational Management*, *26*(1), 83-98. doi: http://dx.doi.org/10.1108/09513541211194392.

Hall, B. & Thompson, H. (1980). *Leadership Through Values*. Ramsey, New Jersey: Paulist Press.

Hall, R. H. (1961). An empirical study of bureaucratic dimensions and their relation to other organizational characteristics (Doctoral dissertation). Ohio State University.

Hall, R.H. (1968). The Concept of Bureaucracy: An Empirical Assessment. *American Journal of Sociology,69* (1). 32-40.

Hallinger, P., Bickman, L., & Davis, K. (1996). School context, principal leadership, and student reading achievement. *Elementary School Journal*, *96*(5), 527-549.

Hallinger, P., & Heck, R. H. (1996). Reassessing the principal's role in school effectiveness: A review of empirical research, 1980-1995.*Educational Administration Quarterly*, *32*(1), 5-44.

Hambrick, D. C., & Mason, P. A. (1984). Upper echelons: The organization as a reflection of its top managers. *Academy of Management Review, 9*, 193-206.

Hambrick, D. C. (1989). Guest editor's introduction: putting top managers back in the strategy picture. *Strategic Management Journal, 10*, 5-15.

Hanson, S. L. (1994). Lost talent: Unrealized educational aspirations and expectations among U.S. youths. *Sociology of Education, 67*, 159-183.

Hanushek, E. A. (1986). The Economics of Schooling: Production and Efficiency in Public Schools. *Journal of Economic Literature, 24*(3), 1141-77.

Harbison, J. R. (1992). Value Orientations and Career Aspirations of those pursuing as MSW degree: Does the BSW make a difference? *Dissertation Abstracts International, 53*(2), 621.

Hargreaves, A. (1994). *Changing Teachers: Changing Times.* London: Cassell.

Harland, J. and Kinder, K. (1997). Teachers' Continuing Professional Development: framing a model of outcomes. *British Journal of In-service Education, 23*(1), 71-84.

Harris, R., Bennett, J., Davey, B. & Ross, F. (2010). Flexible working and the contribution of nurses in mid-life to the workforce: A qualitative study. *International journal of nursing studies, 47*(4), 418-426.

Hawley, W. & Valli, L. (1999). The essentials of effective professional development: A new consensus. In *Teaching as the Learning Profession: Handbook of Policy and Practice.* Darling-Hammond, L. & Sykes, G. (Eds.). San Francisco: Jossey-Bass.

Hazri, J. (2007). Ethnic Arithmetic and The Challenges of Nation Building: A Study of Malaysian Education Policy for National Integration, 1970 to Present (Unpublished Ph.D). Sheffield: University of Sheffield.

Hellrigel, D., Jackson, S.E., Slocum, J. & Staude, G. (2001). *Management – South African Edition.* Cape Town: Oxford University Press.

Henk, W. A. (1987). Methodological concerns in experimental reading research: All that glitters. *Reading Psychology: An International Quarterly, 8*(2), 61-71.

Hersey, P. & Blanchard, K. (1967). *Management of Organizational Behaviour: Utilizing Human Resources.* Englewood Cliffs, N.J.: Prentice-Hall.

Hopkins, D. & Harris, A. (2001) *Creating the Conditions for Teaching and Learning: A Handbook of Staff Development Activities*. London: David Fulton Publishers.

House, R., & Aditya, R. (1997). The social scientific study of leadership: quo vadis? *Journal of Management, 23*(3), 409-474.

Hoy, W. & Miskel, C. (1991). *Educational Administration: Theory, Research and Practice*. New York: McGraw-Hill.

Hoy, W. K. & Sweetland, S. R. (2000). School bureaucracies that work: Enabling, not coercive. *Journal of School Leadership, 10*, 524-541.

Hoy, W. K. & Sweetland, S. R. (2001). Designing better schools; The meaning and measure of enabling school structures. *Educational Administrative Quarterly, 37*, 296-321.

Hsu, T. C. (2011). Enhancing College Students' Global Awareness Through Campus Toastmasters Clubs. International. *Journal of Research Studies in Education,* 21-34. doi:10.5861/ijrse.2012.v1i1.1. Retrieved from http://www.consortiac academia.org.

Hu, L. T. & Bentler, P. M. (1999). Cutoff Criteria for Fit Indexes in Covariance Structure Analysis: Conventional Criteria Versus New Alternatives. *Structural Equation Modeling, 6*(1), 1-55.

Hu, L., & Bentler, P. M. (1995). Evaluating model fit. In R. H. Hoyle (Ed.), *Structural equation modeling: Issues, concepts, and applications* (pp. 76-99). Newbury Park, CA: Sage.

Huber, S. G. (1997). *Head teachers' Views on Headship and Training: A Comparison with the NPQH*. Cambridge: School of Education, University of Cambridge.

Hughes, R. L & Beatty, K. C. (2005). Becoming a strategic leader: your role in your organization's enduring success. San Francisco: John Wiley & Sons, Inc.

Hurlock, E. B. (1967), *Adolescent Development*, New York: McGrow Hill Co.Inc.

Ibn Taymiyah, T. A. A. (1992). *Al-Siyasah Al-Shariyah Fi Islah Al-Rai Wa Al-Raiyah [The Shari'at Politics]*. Beirut: Dar Al-Kutob Al-Ilmiyah.

Isherwood, G. B. (1971). Bureaucracy, alienation and teacher work values (Doctoral dissertation). Rutgers University, New Brunswick, New Jersey.

Jacob, B. A. andLefgren, L. (2004). The Impact of Teacher Training on Student Achievement: Quasi-Experimental Evidence from School Reform Efforts in Chicago.*The Journal of Human* Resources, *39* (1), 50-79.

Jencks, C., Crouse, J. &Mueser, P. (1983). The Wisconsin Model of Status Attainment: A national replication with improved measures of ability and aspiration. *Sociology of Education, 56*(1), 3-19.

John A. Ross & Peter Gray. (2006). School Leadership And Student Achievement: The Mediating Effects Of Teacher Beliefs. *Canadian Journal Of Education, 29*, 3, 798-822.

Johns, R. (2010). Likert Items and Scales, SQB Methods Fact Sheet 1 (March 2010). University of Strathclyde.

Jones, R., A., L. (2004) *Soft Machines: Nanotechnology and Life*. Oxford and New York: Oxford University Press.

Joyce, B. & Showers, B. (2002). *Student Achievement Through Staff Development*, 3rd Ed. Alexandria: ASCD.

Kalargyrou et al. (2012). Leadership Skills in Management. *Education Academy of Educational Leadership Journal, 16*(4), 39-63.

Kaplan, D. (2009). *Structural equation modeling: Foundations and extensions* (2nd ed.). Newbury Park, CA: Sage.

Kaplan, R. M. &Saccuzzo, D. P. (2005). *Psychological testing: Principles, applications and issues* (6th ed.) Thomson Wadsworth. 132-154.

KementerianPelajaran Malaysia. (1988). *FalsafahPendidikanKebangsaan*. Kuala Lumpur: PusatPerkembanganKurikulum, KementerianPendidikan.

KementerianPelajaran Malaysia. (2001). *FalsafahPendidikanKebangsaan, MatlamatdanMisi, Pusat Pembangunan Kurikulum*. KementerianPelajaran Malaysia.

KementerianPelajaran Malaysia. (2006). *PelanInduk Pembangunan Pendidikan (2006-2010)*. KementerianPelajaran Malaysia.

KementerianPelajaran Malaysia. (2011). *PelanStrategik Interim 2011-2020*. KementerianPelajaran Malaysia.

KementerianPelajaran Malaysia. (2012). *DasarPendidikanKebangsaan*. KementerianPelajaran Malaysia.

Kennedy, A. (2011). Collaborative continuing professional development (CPD) for teachers in Scotland: Aspirations, opportunities and barriers. *European Journal of Teacher Education, 34*(1), 25-41.

Keppel, G. (1991). *Design and Analysis: A Researcher's Handbook*, 3rd edition, Prentice Hall.

Kinicki, A., &Vecchio, R. (1994). Influences on the quality of supervisor-subordinate relations: The role of time-pressure, organizational commitment, and locus of control. *Journal of Organizational Behavior, 15*, 75-82.

Kintrea, K. (2009). Aspirations, Attainment and social mobility in disadvantages areas. European network for housing research.

Kline, R. B. (2011). *Principles and practice of structural equation modelling*, 3rd ed. New York: The Guilford Press.

Knight, P. (2002). A systemic approach to professional development: Learning as practice. *Teaching and Teacher Education, 18*(3), 229-241.

Kolesar, H. (1967). An empirical study of client alienation in the bureaucratic organization (Doctoral dissertation). University of Alberta, Edmonton Canada.

Krejcie, R. V. & Morgan, D. W. (1970). Determining sample sizes for research activities. *Educational and Psychological Measurement*, 607-610.

Kutlu, A., & Polat, S. (2011). A *Comparative Analysis of the Perceived Bureaucracy in a Turkish State University*. World Academy of Science, Engineering, and Technology, International Science Index 53, 5(5), 864-873.

Law, K. S., Wong, C. S. & Song, L. J. (2004). The construct and criterion validity of emotional intelligence and its potential utility for management studies. *Journal of Applied Psychology, 89*, 483-496. DOI: http://dx.doi.org/10.1037/0021-9010.89.3.483

Lear, W. (2012).The relationship between strategic leadership and strategic alignment in high performance companies in South Africa (Unpublished PHD thesis). University of South Africa, Pretoria, South Africa.

Leithwood, K. A., Jantzi, D., & Steinbach, R. (1999). *Changing leadership for changing times*. Buckingham, UK: Open University Press.

Lennon, P. (2009). The relationship of bureaucratic structure to school climate: An exploratory factor analysis of construct validity (Doctoral dissertation). Retrieved from http://libproxy.sdsu.edu/login?url= http://proquest.umi.com.libproxy.sdsu.edu/pqdweb?did=2142215831 &sid=1&Fmt=2&clientId=17862&RQT=309&VName=PQ D.

Levine, D. & Lezotte, L. (1990). *Unusually Effective Schools: A Review and Analysis of Research and Practice*. Madison, WI: National Centre for Effective Schools Research and Development.

MacKay, D. A. (1964). An empirical study of bureaucratic dimensions and their relation to other characteristics of school organization (Doctoral dissertation). University of Alberta, Edmonton Canada.

Maden, M. & Hillman. J. (1996). *Success Against the Odds*. London, Routledge.

Maleske, R. T. (1995). *Foundations for gathering and interpreting behavior data*. Pacific Grove, C. A: Brooks/Cole Publ. Company.

Marini, M. M. & Greenberger, E. (1978). Sex differences in occupational aspirations and expectations. *Sociology of Work and Occupations*, 5, 151-174.

Marlow, M. L. (2001). Bureaucracy and student performance in US public schools. *APPL ECON, 33*(10), 1341-1350

McBurney, D. H. & White, T. L. (2007). *Research methods* (7thed.). Thomson Wadsworth. 169.

McCutchen, D., Abbott, R. D., Green, L. B., Beretvas, S. N., Cox, S., Potter, N. S., Quiroga, T., &Gray, A. L. (2002). Beginning literacy: Links among teacher knowledge, teacher practice, and student learning. *Journal of Leraning Disabilities, 35,* 69-86.

Meier, K. J., Polinard, L., & Wrinkle, R. D. (2000). Bureaucracy and organizational performance: Causality arguments about public schools. *American Journal of Political Science, 44*(3), 590-602.

Meyers, L. S., Gamst, G., &Guarino, A. J. (2006). *Applied multivariate research: Designand interpretation*. Thousand Oaks, CA: Sage Publications, Inc.

Md. Afzalur Rahman &DulumoniGoswami. (2013). Level of Aspiration of Undergraduate Students in Relation to Their Sex and Socio-Economic Status. *International Journal of Humanities and Social Sciences, 2*(1), 79-86.

Ministry of Education Malaysia. (2013). *Malaysia Education Development Plan 2013-2025*. Kuala Lumpur.

Motala, E &Pampillis, J. (2001). *Education and equity: The impact of state policies on South African Education*. Sandown: Heinemann Publishers.

Muijs, D. (2004). *Doing quantitative research in education*. Thousand Oaks: Sage.

Muslim, I. A. A. (n.d.). *Sahih Muslim*. Beirut: Dar Ihya Al-Turath Al-Arabi.

Naidoo, S. (2008). The Association between Bureaucratic Principles and Contrived Collaboration: Implications for School Management (Unpublished Dissertation). Faculty of Education, University Of Johannesburg.

Nazifah, A.M (2012). The practices and effectiveness of strategic leadership as perceived by the educational leaders at selected secondary schools in Selangor (Unpublished Master Dissertation). IIUM.

Nasruddeen, H. (2015). Interactive Effects of Principal's Leadership Styles and Quality Assurance Initiative on Teacher Commitment in the Islamic Private Secondary Schools in Southern Thailand (Unpublished Doctoral Thesis). IIUM.

Norazani, A., Jaffary, A. &Hapizah, T. Pendidikan Islam dan Pembentukan Identiti Pelajar: Analisis Dari Perspektif Kaunseling. JabatanFalsafahdanTeknologi, FakultiPengajian Islam, UniversitiKebangsaan Malaysia, Bangi, 2004.

OFSTED. (2000). *Improving City Schools*. London: Office for Standards in Education.

Oluwatayo, J. A. (2012). Validity and Reliability Issues in Educational Research. *Journal of Educational and Social Research, 2* (2), 391-400.

Pandey, S. K., & Kinsley, G. A. (2007). Examining red tape in public and private organizations: Alternative explanations from a social psychological model. *Journal of Public Administration Research and Theory, 10*(4), 779-799.

Pedder, D., and V.D. Opfer. 2010. Planning and organisation of teachers' Continuous Professional Development in Schools. The Curriculum Journal 21, no. 4: 433–52.

Pedder, D., Opfer, V. D., McCormick, R. & Storey, A. (2010). Schools and Continuing Professional Development in England – State of the Nation research study: Policy context aims and design. *The Curriculum Journal*, *21*(4), 365–94.

PenyataRazak. (1956).

Philips, D. C., &Burbules, N.C. (2000). Postpositivism and educational research. Lanham, MD: Rowman & Littlefield.

Pisapia, J. R. & Ying, L. (2011). Values and Actions: An Exploratory Study of School Principals in the Mainland of China. *Front Education China*, *6*(3), 361-387.

Pisapia, J., Pang, N. S. K., Hee, T. H. & Morris, J. D. (2009). A comparison of the use of strategic thinking skills of aspiring school leaders in Hong Kong, Malaysia, Shanghai, and the United States: An exploratory study. *International Journal of Educational Studies, 2*(2), 48-58.

Plucker, J. A. (1996). Construct Validity Evidence for the Student Aspiration Survey.*Journal of Research in Rural Education. 12*(3), 161-170.

Prahalad, C. K. & Hamel, G. (1990). The core competence of the corporation. *Harvard Business Review, 68*(3), 79-87.

Preedy, M., Glatter, R. & Wise, C. (2003). Strategic leadership challenges, in Preedy, M., Glatter, R. and Wise, C. (Eds), *Strategic Leadership and Educational Improvement*, Paul Chapman Publishing, London.

Price, T. L. (2008). *Leadership Ethics: An Introduction*. New York: Cambridge University Press.

Punch, K. F. (1967). Bureaucratic structure in schools and its relationship to leader behavior (Doctoral dissertation). University of Toronto, Canada.

Quong, T. & Walker, A. (2010) Seven Principles of Strategic Leadership. *International Studies and Education Administration (ISEA), 38*(1).

Rabashka, A. and Shepsle, K., A (1972). *Politics in Plural Societies: A Theory of Democratic Instability*. Columbus: Ohio Charles E. Mervill Publishing Co.

Ramsey, R. (2003), *From A–Z: Practical Lessons from Successful Schools and Businesses.* Thousand Oaks: CA: Corwin Press.

Rice, R. (1978). Construct validity of least preferred co-worker score. *Psychological Bulletin, 85,* 1199-1237.

Reissman, L. (1953). Levels of aspiration and social class. *American Sociological Review, 18*(3), 233-242.

Ristapawa, I. &MohdIzham, M. H. (2014). School As Town Council Bureaucracy Unit: A Case Study in Government High School West Sumatera.*JurnalPendidikan Malaysia 39*(2), *141-148.*

Robbins, S., Waters-marsh, T., Cacioppe, R., & Millett, B. (1994). *Organisational behaviour.* Australia: Prentice Hall.

Robbins, S. P. (1998). *Organisational behavior-concepts, controversies, applications.* New Jersey: Prentice-Hall, Inc.

Robison, L. J. (2009). The Importance Of Leadership And Group Facilitation In Learning Communities. *Mcmaster School For Advancing Humanity Journal,* 89-93. Retrieved from http://www.defiance.edulmedia/ McMaster Journal 2009.

Robinson, V. M. J., Lloyd, C., & Rowe, K. J. (2008). The impact of leadership on student outcomes: An analysis of the differential effects of leadership type. *Educational Administration Quarterly, 44*(5), 635 - 674.

Robinson, V. (2007). How School Leaders Make a Difference to their Students. Keynote address to International Confederation of Principals: a paper presented to the 2007 International Confederation of Principals, Auckland, 2 April 2007.

Robinson, S. E. (2004). Punctuated equilibrium, bureaucratization, and budgetary changes in schools. *Policy Studies Journal, 32*(1), 25(15).

Robinson, N. (1966). A Study of the professional role orientations of teachers and principals and their relationship to bureaucratic characteristics of school organizations (Doctoral dissertation). University of Alberta, Edmonton, Alberta.

Rosenbusch, H. S. (1997). Organisationspa "dagogischePerspektiveneiner Reform der Schulorganisation. *SchulVerwaltung, 10*, 329-34.

Rosenthal, R. &Rosnow, R. L. (1991). *Essentials of behavioral research: Methods and data analysis* (2nd ed.). New York: McGraw-Hill.

Ross, J., &Gray, P. (2006a). Transformational leadership and teacher commitment to organizational values: The mediating effect of collective teacher efficacy. *School Effectiveness and School Improvement, 17*(2), 179-199. doi: 10.1080/09243450600565795

Ross, J. A. & Gray, P. (2006). School leadership and student achievement: The mediating effects of teacher beliefs. *Canadian Journal of Education. 29*(3), 798-822.

Rowley, J. (2006a). Where is the wisdom that we have lost in knowledge? *Journal of Documentation, 62*(2), 251-70. DOI: http://dx.doi.org/10.1108/0022041061065332.

Rowley, J. (2006b). What do we need to know about wisdom? *Management Decisions, 44*(9), 1246-57. DOI: http://dx.doi.org/10.1108/00251740610707712.

Salant, P. &Dillman, D. A. (1994). *How to conduct your own survey*. New York: John Wiley and Sons, Inc.

Sammons, P., Thomas, S. and Mortimore, P. (1997). *Forging Links: Effective Schools and Effective Departments*. London: Paul Chapman.

Santhiram, R. (1996). Malaysian Educational Development: A Study of Inter-Ethnic Relations.*Journal of the Institute of Asian Studies, 8*(2), 17- 48.

Scheerens, J. &Bosker, R. (1997). *The Foundations of Educational Effectiveness*. Oxford: Pergamon Press.

Schriesheim, C., Neider, L., &Scandura, T. (1998). Delegation and leader-member exchange: main effects, moderators, and measurement issues. *Academy of Management Journal, 41*(3), 298.

Schoon, I., Martin, P. & Ross, A. (2007). Career transitions in times of social change: His and her story. *Journal of Vocational Behavior, 70,* 78-96.

Schumacker, E. R. & Lomax, G. R. (1996). *A Beginner's Guide to Structural Equation Modeling.* Mahwah, N.J.: L. Erlbaum Associates.

Sekaran, U. (2003). *Research methods for business* (4th ed.). Hoboken, NJ: John Wiley & Sons.

Sekaran, U., &Bougie, R. (2010). *Research methods for business: A skill building approach* (5th ed.). WestSussex, UK: John Wiley & Sons Ltd.

Senge, P. (1990) *The fifth discipline: the art and practice of the learning organization.* New York: Currency Doubleday.

Sewell, W. H. & Shah, V. P. (1968). Social class, parental encouragement, and educational aspirations. American Journal of Sociology, 73(5), 559-572.

Shafritz, J. M. &Ott, J. S. (2001). *Classics of Organization History.* Philadelphia: Harcourt Brace Publishers.

Shamir, B., Zakay, E., Brenin, E., & Popper, M. (1998). Correlates of charasmatic leader behaviou in military units: subordinates' attitudes, unit of characteristics, and superiors' appraisals of leader performance. *Academy of Management Journal, 41*(4), 387-401.

Shanti a/p Rangharan (1998) Peranan Dan Tanggungjawab Guru DalamMeningkatkanProfesionalismePerguruanKearahPencapaianPendi dikanCemerlang (Unpublished Masters Thesis). UniversitiKebangsaan Malaysia.

Sherwood, R. A. (1989). A Conceptual Framework for the Study of Aspirations. *Research in Rural Education, 6*(2), 61-66.

Simon, M. K. (2011). *Dissertation and scholarly research: Recipes for success* (2011 ed.). Seattle, WA: Dissertation Success, LLC. http://dissertationrecipes.com/

Sireci, S. G. (1998). The construct of content validity. *Social Indicators Research. 45*(1-3), 83-117.

Sitra, A. R. A., &Sasidhar, B. (2005). Teachers' Perception on the Effectiveness of Co-Curricular Activities: A Case Study of Malaysian Schools.*UNITAR E-Journal,1*(1), 32. Retrieved from Teo-Education.Com.

Small, M.W. (2004). Wisdom and now managerial wisdom: do they have a place in management development program? *Journal of Management Development, 23*(8), 751-64. DOI: http://dx.doi.org/10.1108/02621710410549602.

Smith, K. B. &Larimer, C. W. (2004). A Mixed Relationship: Bureaucracy and School Performance. *Public Administration Review, 64*, 728–736. doi:10.1111/j.1540-6210.2004.00419.x

Smith, C. L. (2002). Using continuous system level assessment to build school capacity. *The AmericanJournal of Evaluation, 23*(3), 307-319.

Smith, K. B., & Meier, K. J. (1995). Public choice in education: Markets and the demand for quality education. *Political Research Quarterly, 48*(3), 461-478.

Smith, K. B., & Meier, K. J. (1994). Politics, bureaucrats, and schools. *Public Administration Review, 54*(5), 551-558.

Solorzano, D. G. (1992). An exploratory analysis of the effects of race, class, and gender on student and parent mobility aspirations. *Journal of Negro Education, 61*(1), 30-44.

Stacey, R. D. (1992) *Managing the unknowable: strategic boundaries between order and chaos in organisations.* San Francisco: Jossey-Bass.

Stalk, G., Evans, P. & Shulman, L. (1992). Competing on capabilities: the new rules of corporate strategy. *Harvard Business Review,* 57-69.

Strand, S. & Winston, J. (2008) Educational aspirations in inner city schools. *Educational Studies, 34* (4).

Sousa, D. A. (1980). Measuring bureaucracy in schools: a comparison of Hall and Aston Approaches (Doctoral dissertation). Rutgers University, New Brunswick, New Jersey.

Sweetland, S. R. (2001). Designing Better Schools: The Meaning and Measure of Enabling School Structures. *Educational Administration Quarterly, 37,* 296-321.

Syed Ali Ashraf. (1990). Islamic Education and Moral Development I. The Metaphysical Dimension. *Muslim Education Quarterly, 8*(1), 1-5.

Tabachnick, B. G., &Fidell, L. S. (2007). *Using multivariate statistics* (5ᵗʰed.). Boston: Allyn and Bacon.

Teddlie, C., Stringfield, S. & Burdett, J. (2003) International Comparisons of the Relationships among Educational Effectiveness, Evaluation and Improvement Variables: An Overview. *Journal of Personnel Evaluation in Education, 17*(1) 5-20.

Thompson, M. D. (2012). Student Leadership Development and Orientation: Contributing Resources within the Liberal *Arts. American Journal of Educational Research,*1-5. doi: 10.12691/education-1-1-1. Retrieved from http://vubs.sciepub.com/education.

Thompson, C. L. (2003). *Improving student performance through Professional Development for Teachers.* NC: Education Research Council.

Uysal, H. H. (2012). Evaluation Of An In-Service Training Program For Primary- School Language Teachers In Turkey. *Australian Journal of Teacher Education, 37*(7), Article 2.

Vaughter, R., D. Gubernick, J., Matossian, & Haslett, B. (1974). Sex Differences in Academic Expectations And Achievement. Presented At The Meetings Of The American Psychological Association, New Orleans.

Vidoni, D. &Grassetti, L. (2008). The Role of School Leadership on Student Achievement: Evidence fromTimss 2003. The Proceedings of IRC; pg 1-30.

Vockell, E .L. & Asher, J.W. (1995). *Educational research*. Englewood Cliffs, NJ: Prentice-Hall.

Volk, A. (2012). Teachers' Experiences with Bureaucracy in Loosely and Tightly Coupled Systems: Impacts on Professional Practice. Retrieved from http://umanitoba.ca/faculties/education/media/Volk-11.pdf

Walden, U. (2012). Educational social psychology. www.experiment-reserch. com, www.alleydog.com, 1998-2012.

Waters M & Wall D. (2008). Educational CPD: an exploration of the attitudes of UK GP trainers using focus groups and an activity theory framework. *Medical Teacher,30*, 250–9.

Weber, M. (1946). Bureaucracy. Oxford Press.

Weick, K. E. (2001). *Making sense of the organization*. Oxford: Blackwell.

Wenglinsky, H. (1997). How money matters: The effect of school district spending on academic achievement. *Sociology of Education, 70*(3), 221-237.

Wetzels, M., Odekerken-Schroder, G., & Van Oppen, C. (2009). Using PLS Path Modeling for Assessing Hierarchical Construct Models: Guidelines and Empirical Illustration. *MIS Quarterly, 33*(1), 177-195.

Wictor, I. & Andersson, S. (2012). The Importance of Leadership and Vision in Born Globals. *Business and Management Research, 22*(1),13-25. Retrieved from http://dx.doi.ordl0.5430/bmr.vlnlpl3

Wiersma, W. (1991). *Research methods in education: An introduction* (5th ed.). Sydney: *Auyn*and Bacon.

Williams, H. S., & Johnson, T. L. (2013). *Strategic Leadership in Schools*. Education Indianapolis: Then Chula Vista.

Williams, T. H. (1972). Educational aspirations: Longitudinal evidence on their development in Canadian youth. *Sociology of Education, 45*(2), 107-133.

Witziers, B., Bosker, R. J., & Kruger, M. L. (2003). Educational leadership and student achievement: The elusive search for an association. *Educational Administration Quarterly, 39*(3), 398-425.

Wood, Fred H. et al. (1981). *Staff Development/ Organization Development. Designing effective staff development programmes*. Dillon-Peterson, Betty (edit). Association for Supervision and Curriculum Development (ASCD): Alexandria

Worell, L. (1959). Level of Aspiration and Academic Success. *The Journal of Educational Psychology, 50*(2), 47-54.

Worthington, R. L., & Whittaker, T. A. (2006). Scale development research: A content analysis and recommendations for best practices. *The Counseling Psychologist, 34*, 806-838.

Wylie, P. C. (1963). Children's estimates of their schoolwork ability as a function of sex, race, and socioeconomic level. *Journal of Personality, 63*, 202-224.

Yahya, D. (2009). Korelasi dan pengaruh kompetensi emosi terhadap kepimpinan sekolah : perbandingan antara sekolah berkesan dengan sekolah kurang berkesan / Yahya Don. Thesis (Ph.D) – Jabatan Psikologi Pendidikan dan Kaunseling, Fakulti Pendidikan, Universiti Malaya, 2009.

Yucel, C. (1999). Bureaucracy and teachers, sense of power (Doctoral dissertation). Blacksburg: Virginia University.

Zikmund, W. G. (1994). *Business Research Methods* (fourth ed.). Orlando, FL: Harcourt Brace College Publishers.

Printed in the United States
By Bookmasters